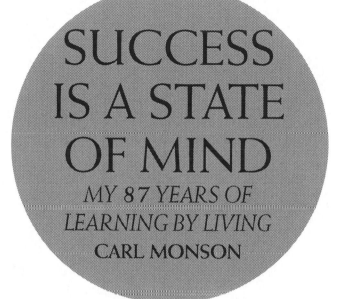

SUCCESS IS A STATE OF MIND

MY 87 YEARS OF
LEARNING BY LIVING

CARL MONSON

authorHOUSE®

AuthorHouse™
1663 Liberty Drive
Bloomington, IN 47403
www.authorhouse.com
Phone: 1 (800) 839-8640

Published by AuthorHouse   07/20/2015

ISBN: 978-1-5049-2365-1 (sc)
ISBN: 978-1-5049-2364-4 (e)

Introduction

Welcome into my life.

This book is my way of telling you about my 87 years on this planet and what I've done to survive and succeed in a changing world.

It's been quite a ride. There have been ups and downs, but overall, it's been a great trip. I think I've learned a few things, along the way, and I'd like to share them with you.

You'll read my life story later, but first, here's "Carl's Code of Conduct:"

Accept full responsibility for your actions.

Learn from your mistakes and your successes.

Select your mentors and friends with great care. Wise people learn from other wise people.

Friendship and trust must be earned. There is no such thing as an instant friendship.

Learn from those who have succeeded, but only if that success has been achieved with integrity.

Richness is determined by who you are, not by how much money you have.

No matter how old you are, you still have a future, so don't waste it.

If life is too easy, you're not being challenged enough to improve yourself.

Relax and laugh as often as you can.

Stay busy, no matter how old you are. Hobbies will fill in the gaps of your idle time.

Be kind to others; it will make you feel good.

No matter how tough it gets, don't give up on yourself.

Your approach to life and the way that you handle your successes <u>and</u> your failures, determine what you will become.

****

My life began on a farm in North Dakota on June 28, 1928. I now live in a small town in North Carolina. During my travels I've been in all of the 48 contiguous states of the United States and in most of the countries of Western Europe.

I've lived on the plains of North Dakota, in the corn country of southern Minnesota, in postwar Europe, and in several of the great cities in the United States and Europe. I've been in the Everglades of Florida and on the rim of the Grand Canyon in Arizona. I've stood at the highest level of the Eiffel Tower in Paris and on the top of the Zugspitze, the tallest peak in the German Alps.

My story will take you through my life in the "dust bowl" and poverty years in North Dakota, living on the farm in Minnesota, twenty years of military service in various parts of the United States and Europe, twenty years of employment in the electronics industry and twenty-nine years of retirement.

Many things have changed in these 87 years.

My family's transportation, during my early years, was a 1924 Chevrolet, without a top; (The top had been blown off during a wind storm.) - - I now drive a modern, four-door, sedan with all of the gadgets that I want to put on it.

When I was a boy in North Dakota, I rushed out into the yard to watch a small airplane as it carried the mail from Fargo to

Bismarck. - - Since then, I've made numerous flights over the United States, Europe, and the Atlantic Ocean, flying in everything from single-engine planes to large jets carrying hundreds of passengers.

I was 14 years old when I first lived in a house that had electricity and the first place where I lived that had indoor plumbing was an army barracks. - - Since then, I've lived in everything from small apartments to trailers and large houses.

My first writing tool was a wooden pencil, sharpened with my pocket knife. - - This book is being written on a computer, using voice recognition software.

Everything in this book is true. Most of it was taken from my memory, but some detailed information was obtained from personal and public records.

Many of the names have been changed to avoid embarrassment to the individuals who are mentioned.

****

As you read, you will notice that I was quite wild during my early adult years, but I got smarter before anyone got hurt. I certainly don't recommend foolishness as a lifestyle.

My birth name is Carl, but early in life I picked up the nickname "Bud." The names are used interchangeably in this book, depending upon where I am at the time of the story.

Throughout the book you will find, *in italics,* my thoughts, and/ or criticisms, concerning places and things being discussed. Please understand that these comments are merely my opinions about what has happened during my lifetime. If you disagree with me, it's all right; we all have opinions about nearly everything.

Chapter 1

A BRIEF LOOK AT MY LIFE

I was born June 28, 1928, in a farmhouse, near Montpelier, North Dakota.

I lived on farms in North Dakota until I was nine years old, when my family moved to southern Minnesota, near a small village called East Chain.

In Minnesota I lived with my parents and, starting at age 13, I worked at various agriculture-related jobs until I graduated from high school on June 1946. College was never mentioned in our house, simply because my parents had very little money and hardship scholarships were not available in 1946.

On June 28, 1946 (my 18th birthday), I enlisted in the Army Air Corps, took basic training in San Antonio, Texas, attended radar school in Boca Raton, Florida, and in May of 1947, was assigned to MacDill Field in Tampa, Florida.

In January of 1948, my parents moved back to North Dakota, where they managed a dairy farm. Shortly after they got there, Dad became gravely ill with pneumonia, so I applied for, and was granted, a hardship discharge from the Air Force to go to North Dakota to help them.

After only one summer in North Dakota we moved back to southern Minnesota. Mom and Dad found work and I hit the road. I never lived with my parents again.

From October 1948 to September 1949, I wandered throughout the United States, surviving however I could. It was adventurous and educational, but not very profitable.

On September 15, 1949, I reenlisted in the Air Force and stayed in the service until December 1, 1967, when I retired. During that time I served at various military installations in the United States, Germany, and France.

I was employed by the American Telephone and Telegraph Company (AT&T) from December 18, 1967 to February 2, 1988, when I retired, again, at the age of 59.

During my retirement years, I've been associated with many non-profit organizations and have traveled extensively.

****

On August 2, 1952, I married Ursula Adele Maus in Wiesbaden, Germany. Ursula died August 8, 1993, in Winston-Salem, North Carolina. Ursula and I have three children, five grand-children, and one great-grandchild.

On January 1, 1994, I married Mary Louise Jackson Jones in Winston-Salem, North Carolina. Mary has three children, and six grandchildren.

Mary and I currently live in Clemmons, North Carolina.

Chapter 2

MY ROOTS

To understand me, you need to know about my parents. It was their morals, their pride, and their work ethics, that taught me how to live and prosper during some very difficult times.

Dad

Gustav (Gust) Monson, birth name, Gustaf Karlsson, was born on March 31, 1895, in the town of Ronneby, Province of Blekinge, Sweden, to Karl Johann Mansson and Matilda Evansdortter. He was the fifth child in a family of six: three boys and three girls. The only one of his siblings to come to America was an older sister, Yohanna (Hanna), who preceded him, and who lived in Chicago, Illinois.

His father died in 1905, and then, when his mother died in 1910, he decided to go to America and start a new life. In 1911, when he was just 16 years old, he made his way to Copenhagen, Denmark, probably by boat, and then boarded a ship named the "Oscar II," bound for New York.

The manifest of the Oscar II shows that the ship left Copenhagen on November 2, 1911 and arrived in New York on November 16, 1911. He is listed as Gustaf Karlsson, age 16, male, single, a laborer and that he could read and write. It also states that he came from Ronneby, Sweden, had $25 in cash, and was to live with the Lundell family, in Chicago, Illinois. He was 5 feet, 6 inches tall and had blonde hair and blue eyes. I remember him as being 2 inches taller and with brown hair, but he probably looked a bit different in 1911 than he did at the time that my memory places him.

After processing through Ellis Island, he went to Chicago, Illinois, to live with his sister, Hanna, and her husband Oscar Lundell, who operated a hardware store. They offered him a job until he could get established in America, so he went to work for them

I don't know how long he stayed in Chicago, but I think he wandered westward, across the western plains, starting in about 1914. He was drafted into the Army on September 4, 1918, in Valley City, North Dakota. He explained to me that he could have refused the draft because he wasn't a citizen, but that he loved his adopted country, and since he planned to stay in America, he was proud to help defend it.

He was assigned to Camp Grant, near Rockford, Illinois, where his duties were that of a prisoner chaser, a man who went after Army deserters and brought them back to the camp stockade.

His enlistment record shows that he was inducted into the Army on September 4, 1918, in Valley City, North Dakota, and discharged at Camp Grant, Illinois, on September 5, 1919. He apparently went back to North Dakota after he was discharged.

His Certificate of Naturalization shows that he became a United States citizen on November 18, 1918, at Camp Grant, Illinois.

He went into the Army, as Gustaf Karlsson, Swedish citizen, and came out a year later as Gustav Monson, US citizen.

There is an easy explanation for the name change:

At the time of his birth, there was a Scandinavian custom that, when people named their children, the children's surnames consisted of their father's given name, plus adding "sson" or "sdotter." His father's name was Karl Mansson so all of the sons were named Karlsson and the daughters were named Karlsdotter. The naming tradition was discontinued sometime about the beginning of the 20th century. To Americanize his name, when he went through the naturalization process he gave them his father's surname, Mansson. The name Mansson, when pronounced with a Swedish accent, sounds very much like "Monson," so when the man who filled out his papers asked him his name, the guy thought that he heard Monson.

As far back as I can remember, he advised me to make a career of the military. His advice was sound

There is a lesson here for all of us who were born in this great country. Immigrants often understand our country better than we do. I'm glad that Dad didn't live long enough to see the unrest during the Vietnam War. It would've broken his heart to see how some Americans acted and how badly some veterans were treated when they returned from that war.

After he was released from the Army he went back out West, working wherever he could, riding the rails, living off the land. Some years, he went to Texas in June, and followed the wheat harvest across the plains, moving northward as the crops ripened. He loved to tell stories of his life as a drifter and I soaked up every word. I suppose that those stories contributed to my burning desire for travel.

My Dad was a 5-foot, 8-inch, 160-pound, giant. He was the hardest working and the most honest man that I've ever known. His physical strength was great and his moral convictions were even greater. He believed that his honor was his most valuable possession, and he lived by that code. I never knew him to lie or to cheat.

Dad died from a heart attack on August 8, 1964 in Fairmont, Minnesota. He was 69 years old.

Mom

My mother, Hazel Belle Mortensen Monson, was born on a farm near Ledyard, Iowa, on February 2, 1906. Her father, Carl Mortensen, was born September 24, 1873, in Denmark and immigrated to America when he was a young man.

Mom's mother, Vinnie Whitman, came from a long line of English and Welsh people that immigrated to the America Colonies in the 17th century.

Mom's family moved to Valley City, North Dakota when she was a teenager. Her mother had died, in Iowa, on May 27, 1912 of lung congestion, caused by the smoke from a prairie fire, and her father had subsequently remarried.

Mom's life was all about her husband and her children. When we were on the farm, she took care of the house, did the cooking and gardening, plus many of the farm chores. But most of all, she was always there for us.

The values of her upbringing were evident every day of her life. I never heard her use a word of profanity, nor take a drink of an alcoholic beverage. She tried to smoke a cigarette once, but after only a few puffs, she couldn't stand the taste of it, so she threw it away.

Mom died from cancer on August 21, 1957 in Fairmont, Minnesota. She was 51 years old.

Mom and Dad are buried in a small cemetery near Ledyard, Iowa.

Their Life Together

In the early part of the last century it was a common practice for a farmer to have a "hired man" and a "hired girl" to help with the work around the farm. They usually lived with the family and were treated very much like members of the family.

In 1922, my father was the hired man, and my mother was the hired girl on the same farm near Valley City, North Dakota. Both of them worked hard, for very little money, but their board and room were provided by the farmer.

One winter day, Dad was working near the barn, when his cap was knocked off by a snowball. He turned around and saw that the snowball had been thrown by the hired girl.

They were married on February 2, 1924, her 18th birthday.

Shortly after they were married, they rented some land near Valley City and began farming. Dad didn't tell me where he got the money for the machinery or the livestock to get that farm started, but somehow they got it up and running. My sister, Virginia Matilda, was born on November 1, 1924, in Valley City.

Their Values

Mom and Dad had very little schooling but, early in life, they taught me that, when times get tough, common sense, and logic, trump education every time. To illustrate; Dad once said, "If you give an idiot an education, you come up with an educated idiot." Simply stated, if you aren't very smart and don't have good common sense, no amount of education will help you succeed in life, but if you are smart, have good common sense, and an education, you will probably be far ahead of the pack.

My parents were a team. They worked together, they played together, and they hurt together. I never heard them argue or raise their voices at each other, and they seldom raised their voices at us children. If punishment was necessary, and in my case, that was quite often, we were punished, but never in anger. As I recall, Dad's belt was used on my back side frequently, but I must have earned the punishment, for I've never held any ill feelings about the way I was treated.

They made the rules and we followed them, it was as simple as that.

For all of the hardship, they never wavered in their love and caring for their children. They never lost their pride, and that pride was instilled in their offspring. We always had food on the table, clothes to wear (often covered with patches), and we never wanted for love and understanding. That's about all that anyone can expect from their parents.

Following are some stories that my father told to me.

Fun on a Motorcycle
Illinois – 1913

When Dad worked in the hardware store, in Chicago, he delivered merchandise around the city using a motorcycle.

He was allowed to use the motorcycle when he wasn't working and he frequently took rides, with a young friend who also had a motorcycle, to Rockford, Illinois, about 80 miles northwest of Chicago. On their way, they often sped through a small town where the local Constable, an old man on a beat-up old motorcycle, had tried to stop them, but never could. They made quite a game of outrunning the old man.

One Sunday, as they pulled their usual prank, they looked back and saw the old man chasing them on a brand-new motorcycle. Needless to say, he soon caught them, and pulled them over. They were pretty scared; for neither of them had any money to pay a fine, nor did they want to go to jail. They need not to have worried. When the Constable pulled them over, instead of writing them speeding tickets, he began to laugh, and then he said, "I should give you tickets, but because you've made such a fool out of me for the last few months, the Town Council finally bought me this new motorcycle. If it hadn't been for you two, I'd still be riding that old relic. Thanks." He waved his hand, turned his bike around, and rode back to town.

They never broke the speed limit in that town again.

Rough Times
Kansas – 1915

One of the problems facing workers in the harvest fields was a labor union called, "The Industrious Workers of the World" (IWW). Dad said that the IWW really meant "I won't work." The union was so powerful that anyone who didn't carry a union card had difficulty finding work. The union men simply walked off the job if a non-union man was hired, so the farmers had no choice but to go along with the union. Dad told me that he carried a union card for a while, but later, after he dropped out of the union, he had several encounters with IWW men.

On one occasion, he jumped into an empty railroad boxcar to ride a few miles, only to be faced by two very nasty looking characters. They asked him if he was a card-carrier, and when he said that he wasn't, they came toward him, expecting to throw him off the train.

What they didn't know was that he was wearing brass knuckles, inside of his leather gloves. When the first man grabbed him, Dad broke the man's jaw and split open his face.

Both men jumped off the train.

He didn't tell me any other stories about the IWW, but I'll bet that there were many.

Working on the Railroad
South Dakota – 1915

Dad was working as a fireman on a railroad locomotive that was climbing a long grade in the hills of South Dakota. He'd been shoveling coal as hard as he could for several hours, but the Engineer kept screaming at him to work harder.

As he approached exhaustion, he summed up all of his energy, and began shoveling as fast as he could, until the pile of coal in the firebox smothered the fire. The train coasted to a stop.

He told the Engineer what he thought of him, jumped off the train, and walked back down the tracks, to the last town that they had passed through.

That was his last job with the railroad.

Frontier Justice
Western Plains – 1916

On one threshing crew, a father and his adult son didn't get along very well. They fought constantly. The son couldn't please the father and the father cussed his son all day long.

One day they were unloading a load of bundles and a fight broke out. The father grabbed his son by the bib of his overalls and threw him into the threshing machine. The son was killed instantly and his body was chopped up along with the wheat.

Several men on the crew, without as much as a word, grabbed the father, and threw him into the thresher.

When the lawmen came to investigate, everyone swore that both men had died when the son lost his balance and fell into the machine and his father had tried to save him.

Nothing more was ever said about the incident.

I guess you could call it an act of frontier justice.

Prisoner Chaser
Illinois – 1918

When Dad was in the Army at Camp Grant, Illinois, his job was to return deserters, Army men who had fled from the camp and had not returned.

On one such trip, Dad had taken custody of a prisoner being held in a small town in Wisconsin and was traveling, by train, back to Camp Grant. Just as the train entered the station at Rockford, Illinois, the prisoner tried to escape by swinging his cuffed hands at Dad's head.

Dad dodged the blow, pulled out his .45 caliber revolver, and whacked the guy on the side of the head, knocking him unconscious. When the train stopped, Dad took the prisoner to the camp stockade, and threw him into a cell.

Dad told me that he had never let a prisoner escape.

Chapter 3

THE EARLY YEARS – 1926-37

In 1926 my parents moved from Valley City to a rental farm near Montpelier, North Dakota.

I was born on that farm on June 28, 1928. Dad once told me that the doctor said to him, "That boy don't need milk, just give him beefsteak." I weighed 10 ½ pounds at birth.

In 1930, Dad bought a 320 acre farm, just a few miles away, using a loan from the North Dakota Land Bank, which processed loans under the Homestead Act, a state law that was passed to help farmers get started during the tough years of the 1930s.

The buildings on that farm consisted of a house, a barn, a chicken house, a pig shed, a granary and a machine shed.

The house had a living room, a kitchen and two bedrooms. There was no electricity or plumbing.

When I was five years old, as Mom was milking the cows one night, she handed me a milking stool and a bucket, pointed to "Spot," a gentle old Holstein, and said, "Boy, it's about time you learned how to milk a cow. I sat down on the right side of old Spot and placed the bucket on the floor under her milk bag. I had watched Mom and Dad milk cows for years and knew a little about what to do so, within a minute or two, I had figured out how it all worked. Everything went well until Spot decided that she wanted to shift her weight from one hind-leg to the other. When she leaned to the right to pick up her left foot, I thought that she was going to fall on me and it scared me half to death.

And so I began to grow up as a farm boy, starting with milking the cows, and moving on to other chores, such as feeding the chickens and other livestock, gathering eggs, and cleaning the barn.

****

To understand what was happening in the state of North Dakota during the 1930s you must look at the conditions during the years of the Dust Bowl and the Great Depression.

From 1932 through 1937 there was very little profitable grain production in North Dakota. Every spring the farmers bought seed and planted it. Most years it rained enough for the seeds to germinate and there was a small harvest, but there was seldom enough rain to produce very much of a crop.

Our survival depended entirely upon vegetables from our garden, eggs and meat from our chickens, milk from our cows, and meat from our calves and pigs. We had a deep well and a 30 foot windmill tower, so we always had water for the livestock, with enough left over to water the garden and to help our friends.

Our deep well became famous, because some of our neighbors watered their livestock at our tank when their wells went dry. For five years, that well supplied water for any farmers who needed water. No one was ever turned away.

If you've seen pictures of the Dust Bowl, you'll have some idea of how we lived. Each morning when the sun came up the wind began to blow and it blew until sundown, sometimes at speeds of 40 mph or higher. The dry ground, coupled with the high wind, created a thick dust storm across the plains, always blowing from west to east. Visibility was very limited and everywhere we went there was dust. Even inside of the house there were little drifts of dust on each window sill. Everything that we ate tasted gritty.

After six years with very little income, there was nothing left to do but to quit. In late August 1937, Dad went to the North Dakota Land Bank in Jamestown and told them that he was leaving his farm, and that everything on it, including the livestock and the machinery, could be sold to pay off the debt that he owed to the bank.

Mom had already been writing to her relatives in southern Minnesota to arrange for a job for Dad and a place for us to live.

When we decided to leave, they arranged for a neighbor, who owned a small truck, to come and help us to move to Minnesota.

When the truck arrived, we loaded it with as much of our personal property as it would hold, then we loaded up our 1928 Studebaker and headed for Minnesota. We never looked back. Several hours down the road, Dad realized that he had left his only dress-suit hanging behind the door in the bedroom, but we had gone too far to go back to get it.

If you have seen the movie, "The Grapes of Wrath," you will recognize the scene. The car was loaded to capacity; stuff was hanging from the outside of the car, and inside were Dad, Mom, Virginia, our dog Queen and me.

We started out just before dark, September 1, 1937, amid the first rain that we had seen in many months.

To learn more about North Dakota read the following stories.

Life in the Dust Bowl
North Dakota – 1934-37

During some of those dust bowl summers there were massive clouds of grasshoppers, numbering beyond count. Some days the grasshoppers were so thick that we couldn't see the sun. The grasshoppers were there for a few days, and when they were gone, there was very little live vegetation left. They even ate the dry pulp from the trees and from the wooden fence posts. There were reports that an airplane, flying out of Jamestown, at 5000 feet, couldn't find the top of the insect cloud. I suppose that this plague was similar to the plague of the locusts, as told in the book of Exodus, in the Bible.

One year, for a couple of days, the land was covered with some type of large, wooly, worms, moving from north to south, eating everything in their path. As they crawled along the ground they never changed their direction. They went up one side of a fencepost and down the other, stripping all dry pulp from the post. When they came to a building wall, they climbed straight up and over the top.

If the building had overhanging eaves, some of the worms fell back down and made a pile at the base of the wall. Again, as with the grasshoppers, when they left, there were no growing plants left.

North Dakota has always had a lot of gophers, big brown ones, not the little striped ones that are found farther east. They lived mostly in the pastures and on the open prairie. They ate grain from the wheat fields, and they had large burrows in the pastures, into which livestock sometimes stepped, injuring their legs. In 1935 the state of North Dakota placed a 3-cent bounty on the tail of each gopher that was killed. Dad bought some steel traps, and he with his .22 caliber rifle and me with my traps, collected hundreds of gopher tails. We stored them in a couple of large tobacco cans and, when the cans were full, Dad took them to town to collect a few dollars to help us buy what we needed.

One day, we discovered that one of the storage cans had been broken into and the gopher tails were gone. Dad suspected that Tiger, one of Queen's grown pups, had found the tails and had eaten them. Dad shot the dog, cut open his stomach, and sure enough, the tails were there. He saved what he could, out of the mess, and returned them to the can.

As you can see from this, in hard times, tough decisions must be made.

Remember, that in 1935, I was just 7 years old.

Early in the dust bowl years, we sold most of our livestock, except for some milk cows and the working horses. We needed the cows for milk and for meat, and the horses to pull our farm implements. There were no tractors in our part of North Dakota until the late 1930s.

Record temperatures for the United States, for both heat and cold, were set in North Dakota in 1936. On July 6, 1936, the temperature reached 140°. By comparison, the highest temperature recorded in Texas, up until that time, was 120°. On the opposite end of the scale, on February 15, 1936 the temperature reached 60° below zero.

We knew that the temperatures were extreme, but I didn't know how bad they were until I checked the records in the World Almanac, many years later.

One memory that sticks in my mind is that of a blackbird, flying against the wind, its mouth open, gasping for air, trying to reach our stock-watering tank. It was flying as hard as it could, but was being blown backward by the wind and the dust.

Our dog, Queen, found out the dangers of the cold when she tried to lick the steel wheel on the barnyard gate. Her tongue became frozen to the metal and she was freed only when Dad poured hot water on the wheel until her tongue became loose. Her tongue was so severely frost-bitten that she couldn't eat for several days.

When I was about six, I decided to find out what the world looked like from the top of our 30-foot windmill tower. I was about halfway up the ladder when I looked down, and there was Dad, his belt in his hand. I scrambled down as fast as I could, but I didn't escape the belt. It seemed unfair at the time, but I suppose that Dad wanted me to grow up to be a man. Somehow I did.

In the summer of 1936 Dad's sister, Hanna, came to visit us. She and her husband had been operating a hardware store in Chicago and had sold out, so they had loaded up their car with useful items and came to North Dakota to see us. One of the items that they brought was a coaster-wagon, the first and only wagon that I've ever had. What a beautiful wagon it was, all red and shiny. I was so proud of that wagon that I nearly burst. I still had it when I was in high school.

On an August day of that same year, we had a small thunder shower; not enough to help the crops, but enough to make the ground slippery. After the shower, I ran, barefooted, across the garden to see if the buds on some flowers had opened after the rain. I leaped over a couple of rows of vegetables, and when I came down, I landed on the jagged neck of a broken bottle, which was sticking up, out of the dirt. The inside of my left foot was cut deeply, about halfway through the main bone. I hobbled into the house, squirting blood at every step. There was no time to get a doctor, and no money to pay for one anyway, so the next best thing was a neighbor lady who had some nurse's training. Dad went for her and she cleaned and bandaged the wound. The rest of the summer I was immobilized, except when my Grandpa Mortensen, who stayed with us for several weeks, pulled me around in my wagon. I still have a large scar on my left foot and my toes don't always bend as they should.

The only car that the family had, from my earliest recollections until 1936, was a 1924 Chevrolet Roadster, without a top. Of course, the top wasn't really necessary because, when it rained, the roads were too muddy to drive on, and in the winter, the car was put in the machine shed until spring. Winter transportation was by a horse-drawn sleigh.

In 1936 Dad received a $150 World War I bonus check from the state of North Dakota and he bought a "new" car, a 1928 Studebaker Sedan. It was already eight years old, but to us it was new.

Another of my fond memories is of the barn in the winter. The temperature outside was often below zero, but the cracks in the barn walls and windows were sealed by frost, keeping it warm and cozy on the inside. The animals lazily lounged about, contentedly munching on hay, or simply dozing. Calves and colts huddled against their mothers, charging up their affection batteries, while kittens and puppies romped about in the straw, not knowing that dogs and cats were supposed to be enemies.

Living on the farm was a great way to learn about life. By the time I was old enough to go to school, I already knew about the reproductive cycle of animals, something that city boys had to learn at the age of 16, in the backseat of a Chevy.

Helping Hands
North Dakota – 1936

The Dalton family lived about 5 miles from where we lived. The farmhouse was a typical two-story, North Dakota farmhouse. The parents' bedroom was upstairs, and on the ground floor, there were 2 bedrooms, one on each end of a large room, which served as a kitchen, dining room, and living room combined. One of the downstairs bedrooms was shared by three girls, ages 11, 9 and 6 and the other one shared by two boys, ages 16 and 2.

It was a cold, wintry morning. The parents had gotten out of bed, started a fire in the wood-fueled, kitchen stove, and had gone out to milk the cows. What the parents didn't know was that, sometime during the night, a gust of wind had vibrated the stove pipe in such a way that it broke apart, up where it went through the roof of the house. Sparks from the fire in the stove started a fire in the attic and within a few minutes the house was ablaze.

The noise of the fire woke up the 16-year-old boy. When he realized what was happening he kicked out the bedroom window, grabbed his little brother and jumped out through the window, landing in a snow bank. He ran to the other end of the house to see about his sisters, but it was too late; the fire had already reached them.

The family lived with neighbors for a few months, and then the community got organized and rebuilt the house and filled it with furniture.

In those days, neighbors helped each other.

Frontier Education
North Dakota – 1934-37

For my first three years of education I attended a one-room schoolhouse, which served the educational needs of 10 to 12 children, covering grades 1 through 8. The only adult in the school was the teacher, a young woman, who was about 21 years old.

The schoolhouse, about 35 feet square, was located on a low hill, some 2½ miles west of our farm. The building was heated by a coal-fired furnace, located in the cellar, with a hot-air duct in the center of the floor above.

There were two toilets on the main floor, one for each gender. (We had two, and only two, genders in those days). There was no running water, so each toilet was equipped with a hole under the seat that opened into a holding tank in the cellar. As you can well imagine, this arrangement sometimes created fragrance problems when the weather was warm, in the spring and fall. In the winter, there were no odor problems, but the hole in the girls' toilet usually became plugged with frozen urine, leaving only one toilet for all of us. I could never figure out why their toilet froze up and ours didn't. I think that it had something to do with the way that they were built. (The toilets, not the girls).

It seemed like we boys were always waiting for some girl to finish using our toilet. I suppose that we were just being trained for the future.

There was no electricity within 5 miles of the schoolhouse. The only water was from a hand-operated pump in the yard.

Going to school in the winter presented some logistics problems and some very ingenious methods of transportation evolved. We walked to school if the weather was good (above zero, and not snowing), but if the weather was bad, Dad harnessed the sled team and took us to school in a covered sleigh.

That covered sleigh had a story of its own. It was basically a 5 feet square by 6 feet tall, wooden box, mounted on cutter runners. It looked a bit like an outhouse on runners; that's probably where Dad got the idea for building it. The entrance was through a hinged door on the right side. A Model-T Ford windshield was inserted in the front wall, with two slots, just under the windshield, to accommodate the reins from the horses. Inside was a built-in bench, long enough to seat two adults and two children comfortably. The sled was pulled by two lightweight, black, horses, sometimes with bells on their harnesses. The silence of the sleigh and the jingling of the bells as we glided over the snow were wonderful. I loved to ride in that sleigh.

And when we got to school, there was our teacher.

Teachers in those little schools typically were very young women, with two years of college, and in their first teaching assignment. Also, they were usually quite attractive. It was rumored that several of the farmers wanted to further their education, but none of them ever did. I suppose that their wives had something to say about that.

If the young lady had been raised in the city, and many of them had, she was in for some surprises when she arrived at her new job.

The first part of a new teacher's initiation came when she discovered that she was required to live with a farm family, down the road a ways, and that she had to walk to school every day. Our teacher was lucky; she lived only about a half a mile from the school.

The next jolt came when she found out that, in addition to being the teacher, she was also the janitor and the furnace fireman.

It took her a while to get organized, but she soon discovered that if she got up at 5:00 AM, had breakfast, and then walked directly to the school, she could get the place warm enough to be comfortable, by the time the children arrived at 9:00. She also found out that if she started cleaning as soon as the kids left, she could be finished before 6:00 PM. and would not miss supper with the family where she lived She graded papers and prepared her lesson plans after supper. She usually went to bed before midnight. *I suspect that teachers were a bit hardier in those days than they are today.*

There were 11 pupils attending school the last year that I was there, enrolled in grades 2-8. The eighth grade was the top grade offered and anyone who wanted more education went to high-school in town. Most farm kids stopped their education after the eighth grade.

Classes were in session from 9 to 4, with a half-hour for dinner. (In those days, dinner was at noon and the evening meal was called supper. Lunch was a snack that the farmers had in midmorning and/ or in the afternoon.) Most of us brought sandwiches for dinner, but when the weather got really cold, the teacher often helped us warm up canned soup that we had brought from home. Someone had donated a two-burner, kerosene-fueled, hotplate and if we brought canned soup, she warmed it up for us.

Keep in mind that she prepared and taught lessons for several students, in up to eight different grades, in one room. Also notice that there was no time for French club, band practice, cheerleading, sports, or any of the other activities that educators today consider to be absolutely essential.

Add to that the problem of teaching one or two children while all the others are idle, and you had a very busy lady. Of course the parents helped by allowing her to punish naughty children when they deserved it. Also, the children understood that a paddling at school usually meant a worse one at home. There were no discipline problems.

Those small country schools should not be compared to the schools of modern times. Not only was the building small, but there was only one teacher. I don't see how one teacher could adequately educate eight grades of children at the same time, but she did. Also, there were no extracurricular activities. Today's schools seem to have much more activity than is really necessary.

Also, farms on the western plains were much larger than in other parts of the country and the population was widely scattered. If those little schools hadn't been there, many miles of travel would have been necessary and transportation was mostly over dirt roads, by horse and buggy or sleigh. Most farmers had an old car but it wasn't driven when the snow was deep.

Dancing at the Schoolhouse
North Dakota – 1934-37

One night, each year, after school let out for the summer, the families of the community gathered at the schoolhouse for a supper and a dance. They came from miles around, to eat, to dance, and to visit with their friends.

Some came by buggy and some came by automobile. Use of the school building was free of charge and the farmers themselves provided the entertainment, so there were no expenses. Everyone brought food and, as if by magic, a keg of beer usually appeared behind the carriage barn. Dad suspected that Mr. Gullikson, the operator of the general store in Montpelier, was the magician. Since the women didn't drink beer, and the children were prohibited from drinking it, the keg was always placed out of sight.

As the crowd gathered, tables were set up, food was brought in, and we ate until the food was gone. The children ate first, the men next, and the women last. To understand this dining order you must understand those saintly, sacrificing, plains women. They always ate last, just in case there wasn't enough food for their families.

About seven o'clock, the instruments were tuned up, the desks and tables pushed back against the walls, the floor was waxed, and the dancing began. Then, except for a beer and smoking break every hour or so, the dancing went on until dawn.

Those dances provided some very lively times. They were times when all of our friends could get together; when our parents could laugh and forget their troubles for just a little while. With so much misery around us, those dances were the only fun that they had.

It was an especially happy time for us kids. We dashed about, slid on the waxed floor, played in the carriage barn, and sometimes caught some teenagers smooching, out among the cars and wagons. As the evening wore on, we children played until we were exhausted, then we found a comfortable spot to lie down and we went to sleep. Children were scattered everywhere; some in the barn, some in cars or buggies, and some under the tables in the schoolhouse.

There was one family who had ten children, ranging in age from two to fifteen. As the dancing began to wind down, about five o'clock in the morning, the parents began rounding up their kids, in preparation for going home.

First, they had to find each of their children, and when they found them, they stood them up and told them to go to the car. But usually the kids weren't awake enough to obey and they just laid back down and went back to sleep. By the time the parents found and woke up the last of the kids, the first ones were sound asleep again. It sometimes took over an hour to round up all the kids and get them into the car. It was quite a show.

One time Dad suggested to them that they should wait until everybody else was gone, then pick up whatever kids were left. He reasoned that a different method of roundup would have saved a lot of work. I suppose he was right, but it wouldn't have been as much fun to watch.

Vern Campbell
North Dakota – 1935

Vern Campbell was a genuine cowboy. He even looked like a cowboy; six-foot-two, wide shoulders, narrow hips. His blond hair usually needed combing, and his sunburned face seldom felt a razor more than once a week. The sides of his boots were scuffed from too much brush-riding, and his heels were worn down on the outer edges. His flannel shirt had frayed cuffs and his jeans were nearly worn through in the seat.

Some folks said that Vern was a bit strange but he seemed alright to me. Mom told me that his father had beaten him with a club, when he was a boy, and that accounted for his lack of smarts. But after all, he was my cousin, so he couldn't be all bad.

Vern was the type of guy who just didn't give a damn about anything. He wandered away from home when he was about 12 and never went back. He shipped out with the Merchant Marine at age 17, and while at sea, off the New England coast, he was nearly killed by a steam-boiler explosion. The explosion made him nearly deaf and from then on, he was as nervous as a fat man in a revolving door.

He made his living using his wits and his natural skills as a cowboy. He lived under the sky and ate only when he could find a cheap meal.

One of his skills was that of a pool player. When he needed money, he just walked into a pool-hall, started a game, made enough money to survive for a week or two, and then drifted on. In those days, every town had a pool-hall full of cowboys, who thought they were experts, so Vern had no trouble making a grub-stake whenever he needed one.

He knew dozens of card tricks and often used them to make a few bucks.

He loved and understood animals. Dad told me that he had seen Vern walk up to the stall of an outlaw bronco, growl some choice words, slap the beast on the rump, and walk into the stall. The animal always moved over to let him in. They understood each other.

He could ride anything with hair on it.

His roping skills were legendary. Using a 20-foot, hemp, lariat, he could rope any part of a horse as it galloped past. If someone called out, "right front leg," Vern snaked that rope out there and grabbed the right front leg of that galloping horse as slick as could be. Of course, as soon as the loop tightened around the horse's leg, he released the rope. He didn't want to hurt the animal. I know he could do that because, one time, several years later, I was riding the horse.

He was about 25 years old the first time I saw him come walking down the road.

Vern spent several winters with us during those lean years in North Dakota. Since he needed a place to stay during the cold weather and he liked us, we could expect to see him about the end of October each year. He usually stayed until spring, helping Dad with the farm work, accepting only his food and his bed as payment, and then, along about the middle of April, he simply packed his knapsack and wandered back down the road. We never knew where he went, but now and then, we received a postcard to let us know that he was alright.

One bright spring day, Vern and Dad were standing in the barn door, watching the horses and cows milling around in the barnyard. It was a warm day and the animals were enjoying the sun after being cooped up in the barn all winter.

Now, I must tell you, that barnyard had <u>character.</u> The snow had melted, but the frost was still in the ground, preventing the melting snow from soaking into the ground. The winter's accumulation of manure was piled about 4 feet high, behind the barn. A thick, yellow river, seeped from the pile. That section of the barnyard was covered with a deep mixture of mud, manure, urine, and water. The remainder of the yard was muddy, but was not as deep.

About 20 cows, calves, and horses were standing on the far side of the yard, munching on a load of hay. Four horses stood about three feet from the barn, almost within reach. Even though they stood ankle-deep in slime, it was warm next to the barn and they were dozing in the sun. (I'll bet that you didn't know that horses can sleep standing up.)

As the two men watched the animals enjoy the sun, the devil got ahold of Cousin Vern. Without saying a word, he went up the ladder to the hayloft, opened the outside door, and jumped out, onto the back of Maude, an old plow horse. He landed on Maude's back, facing her tail, then reached down with both hands, grabbed her flanks just in front of her hind legs, and jerked upward. Now, if you know horses, you know that they go absolutely nuts when grabbed in the flanks like that.

Old Maude was 18 years old and too crippled up to do much bucking, so all she could do was jump up and down a few times, and then just stand there with her head hanging down. Vern swung his leg over her rump, and jumped through the door, back into the barn.

He slapped his leg and doubled over with laughter.

Dad let him laugh for about a minute, then said, "I'll bet you a dollar that you can't do that with old Bob."

Vern looked at Dad for only a couple of seconds, and then spun on his heel and walked toward the loft ladder.

Now, Bob was a mean old bronco, one of those prairie horses with a long, sloping nose, short ears, and the disposition of a rattlesnake. He was worked every day, but he knew, deep down in his heart, that he would never be tamed. He was mean, clean through.

Vern stood in the loft door for a second, then leaped onto Bob's back, and grabbed his flanks.

What happened next was just a blur.

Bob's rump went straight up about 2 feet, and then he arched his back and kicked. Vern was instantly airborne. The horse came down before the man did and when Vern came down, he landed on his hands and knees, directly behind Bob, the seat of his pants pointed at the rear of the horse. Just as he hit the ground, old Bob raised both hind feet and kicked straight back. He caught Vern cleanly in the rump, hoof to cheek, so to speak.

For at least six feet, Vern impersonated a snowplow; his hands and head making a foot-wide trench through the barnyard slush. Fortunately for Vern, the horse's hooves caught him where he was well padded, so he wasn't injured.

At the end of the slide, Vern stood up, wiped his hands on his jeans, and tried to clean the slop from his face. He stood there in the mire and laughed until tears came to his eyes.

Old Bob turned his head and looked at Vern. Old Bob seemed to be smiling.

Dad took Vern to the well and cleaned him up the best he could. It took three washings to get the smell out of his clothes.

A few days later, Vern wandered on down the road and was gone. Dad never did ask him for the dollar.

Queen
North Dakota/Minnesota – 1932-42

Queen was a German-Shepherd puppy that Dad brought home to our North Dakota farm on June 28, 1932 (my 4th birthday).

She was to become a cattle dog, a hunting dog, and a family pet. She was also a good watchdog; protective of us, and hostile toward strangers.

It was a stormy day when Dad brought Queen home. We didn't have much rain during those drought years but we still had violent storms from time to time.

Mom had a terrible fear of wind storms. When she was a girl, she and her family, had been injured during a tornado, and every time a black cloud showed up in the sky, we children were rushed into the cellar for protection.

As the storm rose, Mom herded Virginia and me into the cellar and pulled the trapdoor down over us. The trapdoor had just been closed when I remembered that we had left the new puppy up in the house. I cried and cried, but Mom wouldn't let me go up to get Queen. In just a few minutes, the storm passed and we opened the trapdoor and went up the stairs and into the kitchen. As we entered the kitchen, in the middle of the room was a very frightened puppy and a small pile of dog-poop.

It may seem foolish to go to such detail in describing that scene, but as I write this, over 83 years later, I remember everything very clearly. It must have been very important to me.

Queen lived for over 10 years and gave birth to over 100 puppies. We never knew who the fathers were, for she roamed the prairie and apparently met friends wherever she went. Most of the pups were given away to neighboring farmers, but sometimes we kept a couple and raised them. The rest of the litter was killed. We simply couldn't find homes for all of them, for nearly every farmer, for miles around, had at least one of her pups.

She was a very intelligent animal. She learned quickly and remembered well. Over and over again, she performed tasks that had been explained to her only once.

At the time that I'm talking about, we had about 8 or 10 milk-cows, some other cattle and a dozen horses, all grazing in a 30-acre pasture during the summer. We milked the cows each morning and night and then turned them out into the pasture to graze. When milking time came, Queen trotted out to where the herd was grazing and, very gently, sorted out the milk cows and brought them to the barn for each milking, all without being told what to do. She had learned the routine very early in life and never forgot how to do it. The really big mystery was how her built-in clock told her what time of day to bring them in. Also, she very seldom brought in any cows that weren't being milked.

On a hot summer afternoon Mom was taking a nap and Queen was lying under the kitchen table. A traveling peddler drove into the yard, got out of his car, came up to the house, and knocked on the screen door leading into the kitchen. Just as Mom came out of the bedroom to answer the door, Queen came out from under the table, and with a long leap, hit the screen door at about the level of the man's throat. The man jumped into his car and sped away. It seems that he hadn't learned why farmers had good watchdogs.

One day, Dad spotted a weasel, trying to get some water at our stock tank. He got behind the animal and chased it over to our granary building, under which dozens of rats lived. Within a few days, Dad learned that several of his neighbors were complaining about a large increase in the rat population on their farms and also, we began to find the remains of some dead chickens in the yard. Apparently, our weasel had chased out all of the rats and had started to eat some chickens.

But the weasel made a mistake and ventured out into the yard, where it came face-to-face with Queen. The fight was on. After several minutes of snarling, snapping, and biting, the weasel tried to run away. Queen made a large leap, grabbed the weasel from behind, tossed it into the air, and when it came down, she caught it in her mouth and crushed its head.

****

Queen was in the car with us when we moved to Minnesota in 1937.

****

When Queen was 10 years old, she began to develop lumps in her milk glands. Her spirit was never broken by her illness, but she began to lose weight and her energy faded.

After a few months, Dad had to put her down.

****

Before we leave the Queen story, there is another tale that is worth telling.

When I was 12 years old, Queen had a large litter of pups and we couldn't find homes for most of them. One day when the pups were a few weeks old, as Dad and I were standing in the yard, watching them play, Dad told me that we had to destroy the pups because we couldn't take care of them. He turned to me and handed me his .22 caliber rifle and said, "Can you do it, or should I?" I held my head up high, took the rifle, and walked towards the grove, with the puppies scampering along behind me. When we got into the grove, I killed each one with a bullet to the head. When I had finished killing all those little balls of fur, the tears were running down my cheeks.

Kids grow up early on the farm.

Chapter 4

GROWING UP – 1937-46

Our new home was in East Chain Township, Martin County, Minnesota, where Mom's family lived. This chapter tells about my life in Minnesota from September 1937 to June 1946.

Martin County is located just north of the Iowa state line, about midway between Wisconsin and South Dakota. It's a rural area, with mostly farms and small villages. The exception is the county seat, Fairmont, a city with a population of about 10,000. Most of the businesses there are tied to the farmers and what they produce.

In the southern part of Martin County, on the Iowa state line, is East Chain Township. The village of East Chain is located in the northwest corner of the Township, on the north end of a chain of three lakes. When we got there, in 1937, the village had a Methodist Church, a general store, a barbershop, a café, two automobile garages, a welding and fix anything shop, a chicken hatchery and produce business, a feed mill, and about a dozen houses. Also, on the western edge of the village was the East Chain Creamery, a facility that produced butter from cream that was collected from the local farmers.

Nearly all of the businesses are gone now, victims of modern transportation. (The state paved the road from East Chain to Fairmont.) When I last visited East Chain in 1995, the only business operating was a feed and fertilizer dealership. I was told that it had been there for just a few years. Most of the old buildings, except the general store, the feed mill, and the church, had been torn down. The general store had been operated by various people until, in the early-1990s, it was closed. The Methodist Church still held services every Sunday.

Along the eastern shore of the lake, about a half-mile south of the village, was a place called "bare man's beach." The beach was for men only, but one of the matronly ladies, with a decided lift of her nose, emphatically insisted that women sometimes went swimming there, along with the men. No one dared to ask her how she knew.

Four miles east of the village were located the Swedish Free Mission Church, the Swedish Lutheran Church, and East Chain Consolidated School. The rest of the township was farmland.

East Chain was a good place to live. Everyone knew everyone else's business, but that worked very well. If someone saw a kid misbehaving, they simply called his mother on the party line, and the whole community knew about it, so kids very seldom got into trouble. Also, the system kept errant husbands and/or wives at home. But most of all, if someone needed help, the party line served as an emergency network.

The Olson Farm – 1937-39

The first job that Dad had in Minnesota was that of a farmhand, working for Floyd Olson, who farmed about 100 acres, a mile south of East Chain School. The Olson family lived at the main homestead, and we lived at another set of farm buildings, about a half a mile away. Where we lived there was a house, a barn and a chicken coop, plus other miscellaneous farm buildings.

The house had two rooms, a kitchen and a living room, plus a loft above the living room. Sticking outside, from one side of the living room was a small room, just large enough to push in a double-bed mattress. There was no door on the room, just a curtain pulled across the hole in the wall. That was where my parents slept. I slept on a couch in the living room and the loft was Virginia's bedroom.

The house had no plumbing or electricity, and was heated by a wood-fired stove in the living room. Meals were prepared on a wood-fired cook-stove. The wood for both stoves was gathered, sawed, split, and carried into the house by members of the family. All of the furnishings in the house were either brought with us from North Dakota or given to us by family or friends.

Mom and Virginia did the housework, the cooking, and the laundry. I helped to take care of the livestock, including cleaning barns and chicken coops, and gathering eggs. I also was charged with sawing firewood to its proper length, and then splitting it so it would fit into our stoves. The real heavy work, like cutting down trees and dragging them up for further cutting and splitting, was done by Dad, with whatever help I could give him.

Also, we had a very large garden, raising food to be canned, to provide food for the long winters. That garden always needed tending. Mom, Virginia, and I normally did the garden work. We planted seed, we pulled weeds, and we gathered ripened vegetables, to prepare them for immediate consumption or for canning.

Dad's wages, including the house, were $30 a month. For that $30, he worked from before daylight until after dark, six days a week. He also was responsible for the care of some cattle, pigs, and chickens that were located in buildings where we lived. We were allowed to eat all of the eggs and chickens that we wanted and a couple of times a year, Mr. Olson and Dad slaughtered a pig or a calf, and the meat was divided between the two families.

I know that my description of life sounds like we lived in a pretty harsh world, but it wasn't all that bad. We worked as a family, we helped each other, and above all, we loved each other. Also, as you can well imagine, this upbringing was to set a very high standard for what I did the rest of my life

On the cold, winter days, Virginia often read to me from books such as "The Bobbsie Twins" or played card games with me. Those are precious memories.

The Mulberry Farm – 1940-42

The second job that Dad had was with Lynn Owens who owned three farms that were less than a mile west of where we had been living. The house that was provided for us was on a farm called, "The Mulberry Farm." The farm got its name from the fact that it had over 100 mulberry trees in a grove near the house.

We lived in a wood-frame house with a large kitchen, a small living room, and one bedroom, into which we squeezed two double-beds. Mom, Dad and Virginia slept in the bedroom and I slept in the living room on an artificial-leather, pull-out couch. The house also had an unfinished attic and a dirt cellar. The cellar was where we stored all of our canned goods and whatever else that couldn't survive temperatures below freezing.

When we moved in, there was no electricity or plumbing. We carried our water from the well, and our toilet was an outhouse, about 20 yards from the house. In the winter, our toilet was a pot in the bedroom, except when we were in the barn, and then we did what the cows did.

After we had been there a few months, electricity was installed in the house and the barn. Plumbing was never installed.

An interesting part of the installation job was that the house was over a hundred years old, and when it was built, the walls had been filled with mud, presumably for insulation. To get the wiring throughout the house, the installers had to drill through solid, rock-hard, clay.

About a year after the installation was completed and the power turned on, the house was struck by lightning. The lightning bolt hit the roof of the house, at the ridge line, and the resulting power surge split into two paths. One path went through the peak of the roof and hit the electric line that was strung along the top of the attic. That surge melted most of the wiring in the house, turned all of the light bulbs into dust, and blew the covers off of all the switches and receptacles. The other path traveled down the roof, following a stream of water that fell onto the outdoor antenna that led to our battery-powered radio standing in the living room. The antenna was routed into the house via a metal strip that passed under a closed window. Not only was the radio destroyed, but the rapid expansion of the metal strip, under the window, was so violent, that it shattered the window pane. The radio antenna, which had been strung from the house to a tall tree about 30 yards away, was melted, except for a few foot-long pieces that we found in the yard.

The lightning hit the house about noon. A thunder storm was passing over and I had come into the house, from the garden, and was sitting at the kitchen table. The first sound that I heard was a combination of a loud boom, falling glass, and the clatter of a light switch cover, as its fragments hit the wall behind me. I was quite startled, but not injured. My dog, Queen, who had been sleeping under the bed in the bedroom, came running into the kitchen, yelping, and shaking. It took me several minutes to get her calmed down. After the storm passed, Queen and I walked across several fields to reach Dad, who was working in a field about a mile away. On the way over, I spooked a pheasant from a fence row, and the noise that he made, as he flew past me, just about knocked me out of my shoes. I hadn't realized just how jumpy I was. I trembled for several minutes, and then continued across the field and told Dad what had happened. When Dad got home and we checked the barn, we found that the damage there was minor, but the power remained off until the whole place could be rewired.

The new wiring job took about six months. The workmen had to drill through the clay-filled walls again, since none of the wiring could be salvaged. By the time they were done, Mr. Owens' hired man lived in a very expensive house.

Dad worked in the fields or did other farm tasks from daylight until after dark, six days a week. Mom, Virginia, and I milked about 7 or 8 cows, and took care of the pigs, horses, and chickens. We milked the cows twice a day, and by using a hand-powered machine called a Separator, processed the milk to separate the cream from the skim-milk. The cream was put in a large milk can, which was placed in the cooling tank by the well, to await pick up, two times a week, by a truck from the East Chain Creamery. The skim milk was fed to the pigs. We always held back whole milk for our own use, and sometimes, we kept enough cream to make butter and ice cream. We were furnished all of our meat, dairy, and poultry products. Most of the meat was either salt-cured or, in the winter, kept frozen in a barrel, which was placed on the shady side of the house. During Minnesota winters, the temperature seldom rose above 32 degrees from December through March. Most nights during the winter, temperatures in the low teens and single digits were standard. Several years, it reached about 30 degrees below zero quite often.

We also had a large garden that provided most of the vegetables the family needed.

On Sundays, Dad usually didn't have to work in the fields, but all of the chores had to be done, just the same as every other day of the week.

East Chain Village – 1942-46

In the spring of 1942, Dad decided that he no longer wanted to be a farmhand, so we moved to the village of East Chain, where we lived in a house across the street from the general store. The house had a kitchen, dining room, and living room downstairs and two bedrooms upstairs. There was electricity, but no plumbing.

When we moved to the village, Dad and I began working for Walter Gardner, who owned a chicken hatchery and a feed mill, in the village, and a farm about 5 miles west of town. He also operated a produce business where he bought mature chickens from the farmers and sold them to a slaughterhouse. Dad was paid 35 cents an hour, as a full-time employee, and I was paid 30 cents an hour, part-time. We worked in about every job imaginable. We picked up chickens from the farmers and took them to a slaughterhouse, we vaccinated chickens, we culled chickens to determine if they were laying eggs, and we delivered baby chicks to farmers and to other hatcheries.

Mom also worked for Walt during hatching season, each year, from January to April.

I continued to work there until I finished high school, but I also worked for several farmers in the area.

Mom and Dad worked for Walt until they went back to North Dakota in 1948.

Following are some stories about life in Southern Minnesota.

Life on the Party Line
East Chain, Minnesota – 1937

Let me explain what a party line was. In the early days of telephones, in rural areas, a single telephone line was strung, on poles, along the roads, to provide telephone service to the farmers. Each telephone was a box that hung on an inside wall of a farmhouse. Inside of the box was a transmitting and receiving mechanism and a battery to power it.

On one side of the box was an earpiece, on a cord, and on the other side was a crank, used to send signals down the telephone line. Near the center of the front of the box was a microphone, and at the top of the front were two bells, that rang anytime someone cranked a phone handle, anywhere on the line. There were no dials or pushbuttons in those days.

Each telephone on the line was assigned a series of long and short rings. Since everybody was hooked up to the same wire, a coding system was necessary to identify each phone. The calling system was a series of long and short rings; one turn of the crank was a short, and two turns was a long. For example, if I was calling someone whose code was one short and two longs, I would turn the crank one turn, pause, and then turn the crank two turns. The interesting part of this story is that everyone could hear the rings, and could also hear the voice messages, if they picked up the earpiece.

Since everyone on the line knew the codes for all of their neighbors, whenever someone made a phone call, anyone on the line could identify who was being called, and could listen to the conversation, if they wanted to. It was very common for a farmer's wife to listen to calls that came over the wire. Listening to other people's conversations was sort of a hobby, and it was called "rubber-necking."

Five longs was an emergency call and everybody on the line picked up the receiver and listened to the emergency message.

The party lines are gone now, but the community spirit remains in rural areas such as East Chain. It's sad that more people in this country don't have that spirit.

That was a good system.

East Chain Consolidated School
East Chain, Minnesota – 1937-46

The school, built in 1924, was a brick, two-story building, with electricity and plumbing. Facilities such as electricity and plumbing were quite rare in the rural areas of southern Minnesota at that time. Some farms had electricity, but very few had plumbing. The school also had its own water and a septic system, and was heated by a large, coal-fired, water-circulating furnace. Each room had a radiator or two, which kept the building comfortably warm in the winter. Air-conditioning hadn't been invented yet, so in the spring and fall we simply opened the windows when it got hot. The building contained two restrooms, boys, and girls, both located on the ground floor.

The school served about 200 children, in the 1st through the 12th grades. Basically, the structure was: Elementary School in grades 1 through 6, Junior High School in grades 7 and 8, and High School in grades 9 through 12. The first 6 grades occupied three classrooms, each room with a teacher and two grades of students. Grades 7 and 8 (Junior High) had only one room, with one teacher. Grades 9 through 12 (Senior High) had a home room, which was also the senior high study hall. Senior high classes were held in separate classrooms, depending upon the subjects being taught. The high school arrangement of classrooms and teachers was very similar to that used today.

In addition to the school building, the campus included a house for the Superintendent and his family, a house for the janitor and his family, and a large boardinghouse, called the "Teacherage," where the unmarried teachers lived. The three houses also had electricity and plumbing.

The Teacherage was a two-story, wood-frame building. There were usually about 7 to 10 teachers living there, sometimes including one or two men. I was never in the building, but I think that each of the teachers had their own bedroom, and that the rest of the house was common territory. I have no idea how the cooking, janitorial or toilet activities were organized, but I suppose that they got along, simply because there was no other place for them to live that was within walking distance of the school. Even though a few of them had cars, there were practically no rooms for rent in that farming community. The nearest grocery store was in the village of East Chain, about 4 miles away. Apparently, everyone managed to find transportation whenever they needed to go somewhere. Any teacher that was married found a house to rent somewhere within driving distance.

By today's standards, the administration of the school would seem quite odd. We had only about 200 students, but we were a School District, so we had both a District Superintendent and a Principal. In addition to their administrative duties, those two men also taught some high school classes. I never figured out how the Administration was managed. It seemed to me that we just had two bosses, and they both did about the same things. Discipline was very strict, and punishments often quite severe. There was never any question about who was in charge at East Chain Consolidated School. Mr. John Forrest (JF) Garner was the Principal at East Chain for my last three years of high school.

I was a poor student and if it hadn't been for Mr. Garner and for athletics, I doubt that I would have stayed in school. I simply didn't care about studying. I discovered that I could get by without doing homework, as long as I got good grades on the quizzes and the tests. I rarely did any homework and I aced most of the tests, so I maintained a C average most of the way through high school. I regretted this laziness later, but since my parents didn't know what school grades were all about and they didn't know how poorly I was doing, I got away with it. We all knew that there was no money for college, so that was never discussed.

This is quite ironic considering that, at age 33, I started college at night, got good grades, and received a degree in Electronic Engineering Technology, 12 days after I retired from the Air Force in 1967. I made my living in the electronics industry for over 20 years, becoming a Technical Writing Supervisor within eight years.

The only extra-curricular programs at East Chain were the School Band, the boys' basketball and baseball teams, and class plays, put on each year by the junior and senior classes. I participated in all of those activities.

School Plays - Junior and Senior Years

I guess I was born to be an actor, because I've always liked to show off. The school plays during my junior and senior years were both comedies and I fit into them very well.

School Band

When I was about 10, our parents bought two, used, musical instruments, so that Virginia and I could learn music and play in the school band. I received a clarinet and Virginia received a flute. I often wondered where the money came from to buy such extravagant things. I never learned how to read music, but I learned where to place my fingers on the clarinet keys to match a note that I read on the music sheet. I never mastered the sharps and flats, so I was out of tune most of the time. When I was about 12, Virginia and I played a duet at a church service one Sunday. I still remember how scared I was, and how awful we sounded, but we made our parents very proud. That's all that mattered.

I think Virginia played her flute all through high school, but I gave up band when I became involved in basketball in the seventh grade.

Basketball

The boys' basketball team was divided into two parts: the Second Team and the First Team. For the rest of the story, I'll refer to these teams in the more modern terms of Junior Varsity (JV) and Varsity. Generally speaking, players in the 7th, 8th, and 9th grades, and those older kids who couldn't play well enough to be on the varsity, were on the junior varsity. In a small school like this, there were not enough players to form two full teams, so the starting five of the JV team were on the bench (subs) for the varsity.

The schedule was such that on any given night there were two games; a JV game followed by a varsity game. With this situation, it was possible that a JV player could play two full games in one night if a varsity player was injured or was not performing well.

In the seventh grade I found out about basketball. I can still remember the first time that I entered a game. I was setting on the bench when the coach looked over and told me to go in, so I jumped up and ran out onto the floor. I didn't know where to go, but Bob Knight, a ninth grader, pointed to a spot on the floor and said, "Stand over there." So I stood over there, and then I ran around the floor trying to figure out what was going on. I don't remember very much about the rest of that season.

In the eighth grade I played on the JV team, even starting a few games. As a freshman, I was a starter on the JV team and a sub for the varsity.

Early in my sophomore year, one of our regulars, a senior, was drafted into the Army, and I was promoted to the starting lineup of the varsity. That's where I was for the rest of the time that I was in high school.

I know it seems odd that a boy only 5'9" tall could play the position of Forward on a basketball team, but this was a small school and the tallest kid in the school was 6'2". It was quite difficult to play against a 6'6" Center or Forward, but I often did. As you can imagine, we didn't have a very good basketball team. We played in a conference made up of mostly small schools like us, but there were some schools that had several players that were much taller than any of us. Because of the size difference and because I was very aggressive, I fouled out of many games. It seems that the referees didn't understand that the only way that I could get above those guys was to crawl up their legs or to grab their arms.

I was a good shooter and in many of the games I was the leading scorer. In those days, high schools played 8-minute quarters, and each player was allowed only three personal fouls per game, consequently, most of the games were low-scoring, with neither team scoring more than about 40 points.

In one memorable game, we played a school with even less talent than we had, and I scored 26 points. Since the Fairmont Daily Sentinel had people calling in scores from all over the area, they picked up on my outstanding performance. They built a big story out of what I had done and compared it to a game that Truman Hi had played the same night, in which their Center also scored 26 points. To add to the hype, East Chain was scheduled to play Truman the next week. Well, in that game, the Truman Center scored about 35 points and I had four. My tenure as a Star lasted just one week.

With all the ups and downs, basketball was a very important part of my life during those years. Four years after I graduated, while stationed with the Air Force in Germany, I played for a couple of years, but never played after that.

Baseball

I played baseball during my junior and senior years, playing at various positions, but mostly pitching. I didn't enjoy playing baseball as much as I did basketball, but I had a good time, played in every game, and earned a Letter in the sport, all three years.

You may notice that the problem of discipline is not mentioned in this conversation about schools. It's because there were no discipline problems in any school that I attended. It's quite obvious to me that the major difference between then and now is that the parents took care of the discipline in the old days. If any kid got in trouble, a note was sent home to the parents, and the child was punished by the parents. Apparently that system no longer works.

Master of Education
East Chain School – 1943-46

John Forrest Garner, the principal of East Chain School, was a very special person. He was a farm boy who had worked his way through the State University of Kansas. As a farm boy himself, he understood the problems of farm children like us. He knew and loved every student in the school, and he made it a point to know their parents as well.

He was a rather small, very neat, very intense man, in his late forties. He always wore a three-piece suit, even when the weather was hot. His personal standards were high and he set high standards for the teachers and the students.

Mr. Garner was the principal of all twelve grades, but most of his work was with the junior and senior high school students. The first six grades, because of the closed environment in which they studied, needed very little of his personal attention.

In the many years that I knew him, I never saw him raise his hand or his voice against a student. All of the students knew that Mr. Garner loved them and they also knew that if they misbehaved, he would take away some privileges. His word was the law, and everybody knew it. He was a father-figure to many of us.

Mr. Garner firmly believed that every student could be successful at whatever they set out to do. He understood the abilities and the attitudes of everyone and helped them attain the maximum knowledge possible. Any student who didn't earn passing grades simply didn't pass the class. There was no coddling of students in his school. I know, because I was one of the most rebellious and troublesome students that he had. But Mr. Garner never gave up on me. He pushed and prodded and pleaded, until I began to learn, in spite of myself. He would not let me fail.

Two years after I graduated, while on leave from the Air Force, I visited with Mr. Garner. I sat down next to his desk and we talked for about an hour. At one point, he looked up at me and said, "Carl, you could have been the valedictorian of your class, if you had applied yourself." I know that he was just being nice to me, but it was a lesson that I've never forgotten.

He made me realize that if I had worked to my full potential, I would have had a much better life.

Mr. Garner died in a nursing home in Fairmont, Minnesota many years ago.

Working for Pay
Southern Minnesota – 1941-45

Keep in mind, as you read this, that the World War II military draft started in mid-1941 and from that point, until the autumn of 1945 most of the able-bodied men, below age 40, were serving in the military. It was a sad time for the country, but because I was a big, strong kid, I could find work any time that I wanted to. I was hired to do a man's work most of the time that I was in high school.

I had worked on the farm, along with my father, from the time that I was a small boy, but at age 13, I became mature enough to get paid for my work.

Most teenagers today are given an allowance. I was "allowed" to live in our home, as long as I did my chores.

****

Lynn Owens owned three large farms on which he produced corn, oats, and potatoes. Dad worked for him for three years and we lived in a house on one of his farms.

On the farm, where we lived, there was a dried-up lake bed of about 30 acres. The topsoil in that lake bed was a 10-foot-thick layer of very rich, black, fine-grained mulch, which was perfect for the growing of potatoes.

The summer that I was 13 years old, Mr. Owens decided to try his hand at raising carrots. He planted about 15 acres of carrot seed in the lake bed and as soon as the carrot sprouts were above ground, my sister, and I were hired to keep the patch weeded all summer. We worked, side-by-side, on our hands and knees, for 10 hours a day, six days a week. Virginia was paid one dollar per day (she was four years older than me), and I was paid 75 cents per day. That was the first money that I had ever earned and I saved most of it.

After the carrots were harvested, Mom took me to the Montgomery Ward store in Fairmont, and I bought a bicycle. I didn't spend all of the money that I had, but I bought the finest bicycle that I had ever seen. I think I paid $34.95 for it. Just think of it, I'd never owned anything in my life, and now I had a new bicycle, with white sidewall tires, fenders, wide handlebars, and reflectors on both the front and the back. I thought that I was in heaven.

In September of the same year, I was hired to pick up potatoes during the potato harvest. The potato-picking crew followed the digging machine and picked up and bagged the potatoes for ten cents a bushel. The first day that I worked, I earned about two dollars. (A good picker could pick 100 bushels a day and earn about $10.00.) I lasted less than a week. I wanted the money, but school had started the day before I went to work, and after a couple of 10-hour days and an aching back, I decided that I needed an education more than I needed money. I quit work and went to school.

****

Starting with the year that I was 14, I began to branch out and I worked for anyone who would give me a job. I worked wherever and whenever I could, as long it didn't interfere with my school activities.

I was in high demand as a worker. I learned how to operate most of the equipment, and the farmers knew that they could trust me in the fields with minimum supervision. Quite often, during the busy seasons, farmers came to East Chain School, and asked for me, and I'd work for a day or two. My parents knew about these arrangements, so the school Principal allowed me to leave school to go to work.

Poultry & Milling

In the village of East Chain, Walter Gardner owned a chicken hatchery, a feed mill, and a poultry marketing business. Those operations provided me with part-time employment throughout the year. Dad worked for him full-time, and Mom and I worked part-time. Mom and Dad got paid 35 cents an hour and I got 30 cents.

On weekends and a couple of nights a week, during January and February, I loaded trays of eggs that were placed into the hatchery incubators and then helped the crew that took the baby chicks out of the incubators and placed them in boxes, to prepare them for sale to local farmers.

Since the farmers who bought these chicks were buying them for use in breeding flocks, they bought only female birds. So, twice a week, on the day that a batch of chicks came out of the incubator, a team of men came to the hatchery to examine each chick to determine its gender. The processing was called "sexing," and here's how it worked:

A box of chicks, each containing about fifty babies, was placed on a table and a man picked up each chick, turned it over and looked at its rear-end, determined the gender of the chick and tossed the bird into one of two boxes, one for each gender. The females were sold to the farmers and the males were destroyed.

****

One Saturday night, while the sexing was going on, one of the local farmers happened by and stooped over, hands inside the bib of his overalls, to watch what was going on. After watching for a while, he asked the worker, "How do you know which is which?"

The worker looked up at the farmer and said, "If it winks at you it's a girl."

The farmer replied, "Well, I'll be damned." Then he turned and walked out the door.

Sometimes education is quite humorous.

****

The farmers bought ten-day-old chicks from the hatchery and raised them, using feed that was purchased from the mill. When they were old enough to breed and start laying eggs, the hatchery brought in highbred roosters (one roster per ten hens) from outside of the area, and placed them in the flocks. In this way, no cross-breeding occurred, which might have contaminated the blood line. Then, the next year, the farmers sold the eggs back to the hatchery, and a new crop of chicks were hatched.

Another part of the operation was that of maintaining the health of the flocks that provided eggs to the hatchery. I worked in the early part of every summer, helping my Dad vaccinate entire flocks, sometimes containing several hundred birds, against various chicken diseases. The processes are too complicated to discuss here, but since we had to handle every chicken, it was hard, dirty work.

There is a process, called "culling," to determine if a hen is producing enough eggs to earn her keep. There is a method of determining, by checking a bird's physical structure, if she is producing eggs. Dad knew how to make the diagnosis, so we culled chicken flocks and bought the non-laying hens, to ship to a slaughterhouse. We were told by several farmers that we were so good at what we did that, after we had culled their flocks, they couldn't notice any decrease in egg production.

The mill received truckloads of grain, brought in by the farmers, ground it into whatever consistency the farmers wanted, then mixed in vitamins, oils, and minerals to prepare it for use as livestock feed. After mixing, the prepared mixture was loaded back onto the truck. That was a very dangerous and dusty place to work. The machine was operated by a full-time employee, but I helped unload the trucks and carried around hundred-pound bags of materials that were mixed into the grain.

Throughout the year, whenever I wasn't working for Walt, I was on-call to work for several farmers in the area, as described below.

General Farm Labor

My farm work consisted of driving tractors or horses, and doing just about any job that was done on a farm. During the school year, from September through May, I worked mostly on weekends and after school, doing chores around someone's farm whenever I was called. During the summer months I worked 6 days a week.

Individual tasks depended on who was working on any giving day, and who had the most expertise in the particular part of the job.

Harvest Time

The small-grain harvest began in mid-July and lasted about three weeks. The harvesting of grain was much different in the 1940s from what it is today.

Let me tell you the differences, and as I go through this, keep in mind that I was doing most of the jobs described in this process.

This is the way it worked:

Each farmer had his own binder, pulled by either a tractor or by four horses, which cut the grain and tied it into bundles, which were dropped behind the binder in the field. The next day, men came and stacked the bundles into little tepee-shaped shocks of about eight bundles each, with the heads of the grain pointed upward, so that the grain-heads could dry before being threshed.

A couple weeks later the threshing operation began. Usually, one threshing machine, owned by one farmer, would process the crops of about 10 farms, moving from one farm to the next, until all of the farms had been served. It was a cooperative effort, and each farm provided some of the men and machinery to complete the operation.

The threshing of the grain, to separate the grains from the straw, was done by a large, belt-driven, machine called a threshing machine. The job of hauling the bundles to the threshing machine was performed by about 10 men, each driving a two-horse team, pulling a bundle rack. Each man loaded his rack, took it to the threshing machine, and unloaded it, throwing the bundles onto the conveyor belt that fed the machine. Then he went back out, got another load, and repeated the cycle.

The threshing machine began operation each morning when the dew was gone from the grain shocks, and it operated until sundown, with a one hour break at noon, so the men could eat dinner. Supper was served after the day's work was done, and then the men drove their bundle teams, with their racks, home for the night.

In addition to the bundle hauling crews, there were several men who hauled the grain to the granaries and who operated and maintained the equipment.

All in all it was a very large and complicated operation.

One thing that could be said, about harvest time, was that the men were served great meals. Wherever the machine was set up, that farmer fed all of the men two meals a day, both dinner and supper. The ladies of the host families competed to see who could prepare the best meals for the men. We worked hard but we were always treated well and fed well.

I was a bundle hauler for two summers, working for the man who owned the threshing machine. I was paid 3 dollars for each 10 hour day that I worked. Those were the summers that I was 16 and 17 years old.

Since my day, the modern combine, operated by one person, has replaced all of the men, the machines, and the other equipment involved in the harvesting process described above.

The preceding section described my work when I was a teenager. That was the beginning, and from that came my basic concept of what it takes to succeed in life: Your supervisor tells you what to do, he helps you learn the skills, and then you do the work. Personalities don't enter into the equation. At some point in our working lives we have all had some bosses that we didn't like, but if we wanted to get paid, we worked through it or we quit the job and found another one.

If your boss decides that you can't do the job, you get fired, or maybe, if he likes you, he will help you find a spot somewhere else in the same company. The point that I'm trying to make here is that, if you want to be employed, suck it up, and wait for something to happen.

A Couple of Nice Old Guys
East Chain, Minnesota – 1942

In the Hopalong Cassidy western movies, Hoppy had a sidekick named Andy Clyde. You remember him, don't you? Little guy, bowed legs, rundown boots, ragged hat, scraggly mustache drooping over the corners of his mouth. He squinted, and when he laughed, he cackled.

Well, Andy Clyde had a look-alike in East Chain. Lou Owens was about 5 feet, 5 inches tall, thin as a rail, and had skin the texture and color of tanned leather. He had thinning, gray hair, and a full, gray mustache that drooped at the corners. He looked like a very old, tired, cowboy, but he wasn't. I never did figure out what he was. Mostly he was just a nice guy that I knew in East Chain.

Lou had a good friend named "Hoot" Schoeder. They were buddies, but they were a very unlikely pair. Hoot was over six feet tall, with a large belly and lots of hair.

They did nearly everything together. Neither of them did any more work than was absolutely necessary, so they had plenty of time for their favorite pastimes; drinking beer and playing cards. Most of all they liked to play poker with their favorite playing pal, Pete, whose farm was over across the lake. There were two ways to get to Pete's place; drive three miles around the lake or go one mile across the water. In the summer, they usually went in Hoot's boat, and in the winter, Hoot drove his car across the lake on the ice. Every winter the ice was over two feet thick, so driving a car across the lake was no problem.

One nice, warm morning in early March, Hoot picked up Lou in his old Ford and they drove across the lake to see if they could separate Pete from some of his money.

They played and drank all day and about 4:30 they staggered out of the house and crawled into the Ford for the trip home, across the ice. Hoot coaxed the car to life, stuck a fresh plug of tobacco inside of his right cheek, and headed across the lake, doodling along at about 15 miles an hour. Lou was sprawled out across the back seat, nearly asleep.

They had gone nearly halfway across the lake, when Hoot, through the blur of his drunkenness, realized that he was looking at open water instead of ice. The ice had started breaking up in the warm spring air, creating a gaping hole in the ice about a hundred yards ahead.

Hoot swallowed his chewing tobacco, let fly with a few choice, non-Christian, words and started spinning the steering wheel. The car began to spin, still sliding toward the open water.

The good Lord must have been looking out for old drunks that day, because, on the fifth cycle, the car quit spinning, facing away from the open water.

The commotion awakened Lou. He jumped up, spun around in the back seat, and stared out the back window. All he could see was rippling water coming toward him at a terrifying speed.

"Hoot, Hoot, Hoot," He screeched, "We ain't agonna make it Hoot, we ain't agonna make it Hoot." His face had turned as white as a preacher's Sunday shirt. He was sure that he was going to die and in his hazy mind he worried about dying without sobering up first.

Hoot's mind apparently cleared up some, because he eased up on the accelerator and the wheels stopped spinning enough for the tires to get better traction. The car slid to within about twenty feet of the edge of the ice, then gradually began to inch its way forward again. Lou had fainted and didn't know that they were safe.

They made their way around the open water and arrived home safely. They didn't drive on the ice again until the next year. They even quit drinking beer for nearly two weeks.

Mabel Owens noticed a change in her husband, and sort of hoped that he would get religion. But after a few weeks, he was back to his old habits.

****

Lou's wife, Mabel was the president of the local chapter of the Women's Christian Temperance Union, usually referred to as the WCTU. She was a pillar of the community.

In the basement of their house, two projects were underway, one known to nearly everyone, and the other one known only to Lou.

Mable had made six crocks of sauerkraut, and it was fermenting, just like it was supposed to. By the smell, you could tell that it was going to be an excellent batch.

Because her knees hurt when she climbed stairs, Mabel didn't go down into the basement unless she had to.

Lou knew of his wife's reluctance to go into the basement, so he decided to do a little fermenting of his own. He made ten bottles of homemade beer and hid them in two empty crocks that his wife hadn't used. He put lids on the crocks and placed them next to the kraut crocks. He reasoned that if his wife ever went into the basement, she would think that all of the crocks were full of kraut. It darn near worked.

On a Thursday afternoon the WCTU was meeting in Mable's living room. The meeting was going well. The eight ladies had spent nearly three hours discussing and viciously condemning the use of the Devil's brew by the no-good men of the community. No names were ever mentioned at those meetings.

They had just finished the closing prayer, when all hell broke loose. It seems that Lou's beer recipe had some flaws in it. All ten bottles went off in about five seconds. A couple bottles exploded with such violence that they broke a kraut crock and its contents spilled onto the floor. It took about 30 seconds for the odor to reach the WCTU ladies upstairs. I must tell you that fermenting sauerkraut and rotten beer do not combine well.

The ladies fled for their lives.

It's not necessary to mention that Lou was in disfavor at home for quite some time. It didn't help, when the fair ladies of East Chain voted to remove Mable from her position as president of the WCTU.

It's a sad world. Just a few months before, the Lord had saved Lou from drowning; now the Devil was actively working against him again.

Uncle Roy
East Chain, Minnesota – 1942

My Uncle Roy Conklin was my great-grandfather's half-brother. The first time I ever saw him he was over 80 years old and had just retired from his ranch in western South Dakota. He had moved to East Chain to be near his family during his declining years. It was the first time he had been back east since he had gone to South Dakota when he was a young man.

Roy was five feet, six inches of muscle, blood and guts. He was nearly three feet wide, but there was no fat on that old body. His health was excellent.

I liked him instantly.

His stories of life on the frontier were truly fascinating to me. To hear his tales, I visited his house every chance I had. He never disappointed me.

He talked of the times that he fought renegade Indians who had killed ranchers and stolen their cattle and sheep. He related how he had joined a sheriff's posse to round up a gang of rustlers. His life was like a dream to me. He talked only of the interesting times, however, and never mentioned the times that life were just plain hard work. It never occurred to me there were rough times in the old west. Uncle Roy just never mentioned them.

Roy had a hard time adjusting to retirement. Anyone who had worked as hard as he had couldn't just sit in a rocking chair for the rest of his life. He was constantly on the move, walking around the village, visiting with anyone who would talk to him.

The East Chain Restaurant was a little coffee shop that served snacks and lunches. Since it was open all day, and since there was no other place in the village that served free coffee, it was a natural place for retired gentlemen to congregate. On any given day, anywhere from two to a half-dozen retired men could be found playing cards at the restaurant.

The two most regular players were Uncle Roy and a retired Polish farmer named John Petleski. Those two and several other old men had been playing poker, a couple times a week, for many years.

A potential problem always existed when these two old pirates played cards. You see, each of them had so much pride that he couldn't bear to lose, consequently, they both cheated all the time. No one dared to accuse them, and the other players enjoyed the rivalry, so the games went on, uninterrupted. There was very little money involved, so no harm came to anyone.

They had played cards in this fashion for nearly 10 years. Roy was not quite 90 and John was about 85, when an incident occurred that destroyed their friendship.

Roy caught John with an ace in his vest pocket.

Roy jumped up from the table, spilling cards and coffee on the floor, and pointed his finger at John.

"You old son-of-a-bitch," he shouted, "You've cheated me for the last time. Come on outside and I'll whip your ass." Roy stomped out the door and into the street.

Poor old John was too startled to move, but then his pride took over and he headed outside, followed by four other men.

The two squared off, each striking "John L. Sullivan" poses. They circled around and around in the dirt street, neither attempting to throw a punch. The card players cheered them on. These old guys hadn't seen a fight in a long time. It was a nice break in the dull routine of retirement.

Finally, after several turns of the circle, Roy managed a jab with his left hand and grazed John's right cheekbone. Blood began to flow down John's cheek.

I suppose that the sight of blood made the onlookers realize that someone might get hurt, so they grabbed the two gladiators and held them apart. John pulled a handkerchief from his overalls pocket and held it to his bleeding cheek. He looked around at his circle of friends, then got in his car and went home.

Roy, the fight gone out of him, was led back into the restaurant. After several minutes, all of the men went home.

It was over a year before John Petleski came back to the card games, and then, it was never quite the same again. There was always a tension in the air whenever he and Roy played in the same game. Both were too strong willed to admit they were wrong and neither ever apologized.

The last time I saw Uncle Roy he was 97 years old. He was very unhappy. He told me that all of his friends were gone and he didn't have any reason for living. I tried to comfort him, but only partly succeeded.

Roy Conklin died in his 101st year.

Outhouse Capers
East Chain, Minnesota – 1943

This story discusses outhouses. It's a very complex subject, so for you city slickers, and for those of you born after 1945, I'd better explain what an outhouse was.

The primary function of an outhouse was that of a toilet, but as you will see in this story, it was also sometimes the source of laughter and of riotous behavior. An outhouse was a necessity for rural folks who didn't have plumbing in their houses. City folks who didn't have indoor plumbing had their own problems. I won't go into that.

Since this is a very scientific discussion, I must go into quite some detail about the construction and usage of an outhouse.

If you really have a great interest in this subject, go to Google and simply put in the word, "outhouse" and be prepared to learn and to laugh. ☺

But as you do that, keep in mind that I'm talking about the good ol' days.

The construction was of wood, nailed together with iron nails, although some older models seemed to be held together by nothing but several layers of paint. A typical outhouse was a box-shaped structure, 7 feet tall, 5 feet across, and 4 feet from front to back. The roof was sloped, usually from front to back, and was covered with wooden shingles. The structure had a front door, large enough for the largest member of the family to pass through, when in a hurry. The door was equipped, on the inside, with a metal spring and a hook, to ensure that the door stayed closed, even in a high wind. The windows were covered with screen or glass and were only large enough to allow adequate lighting for the reading of old Sears and Roebuck catalogs or other such high-grade literature.

A 2 by 2 foot bench-seat was nailed across the inside of the back wall, 2 ½ feet from the ground. Cut into the bench were two round holes. One hole was cut to fit the rump size of the largest member of the family and if they had children, the other hole was smaller, to accommodate their dimensions. A wooden panel was then nailed in place, to cover the open space between the seat and the ground. Then a floor was installed. For obvious reasons, the floor was omitted underneath the bench seat. Before the outhouse was placed in its permanent location, a hole, 4 feet long by 2 feet wide by 5 feet deep, was dug in the ground, several yards from the house. The outhouse was then moved over the hole so that the hole received the deposits from the customers of the outhouse. (Much like the letter drop at the post office that receives your income tax return.)

Of course, after several years, the hole filled up and a new hole had to be dug and the building moved to its new site. This operation was code-named, "moving the smokehouse" just in case some ladies were listening on the party line when it was discussed. For example, if I received a call from Charlie and he asked me to help him move the smokehouse, I knew that I was to get a few bottles of beer and come to his place for an afternoon of hard work. Without the beer, the task would have been nearly impossible.

****

George Tobin was one of the great practical jokers of all time. He had never hurt anyone, but he had played some pretty nasty jokes on his friends from time to time. Now, he was getting old and wasn't as active as he once was, so some of the younger folks mistakenly believed that they could get even.

George had lived alone on his farm for several years, since his wife died, and his daily routines were pretty regular.

His farm was quite ordinary, with a house and barn, some other buildings, and a standard, genuine, American outhouse, located about 100 feet due east of the house. The easterly direction was necessary because the prevailing winds in Minnesota are from the west. Also quite ordinary was the fact that George went to the outhouse every night just before bedtime. It was dark out in the yard, but since George had made the pilgrimage each night for over forty years, he needed no help in finding his way.

Well, one Halloween night, about ten o'clock George made his nightly trip to the outhouse. He was quite intent on where he was going and didn't see the three Whitman boys back in the trees watching him. He probably should've heard their snickering, but he was bent on his mission and didn't pay much attention to what was happening around him.

As soon as he was inside, the boys rushed forward and tipped the building forward, with the door on the downward side. Since there was only one door and the windows were much too small to crawl through, George was trapped. He screamed a few words, known only to the Devil and to old farmers; but the Whitman boys were already gone.

In the morning, Archie Whitman called George's closest neighbor, Frank Pierce, on the party line, and told him about the prank. Frank and one of his boys went over and tipped the outhouse back upright and let George out. Within hours, everyone in the township was aware of the prank and had a good laugh at George's expense. Someone had finally gotten even with the "master prankster."

Now, George was old but he wasn't senile. He wasn't about to let those Whitman boys get the best of him, so he planned his revenge.

The boys were planning too. They figured that he wouldn't expect them again, so they decided to play the same stunt again the next year. They should've known better.

Halloween night came, and sure enough, there they were, waited in the trees until George came to the outhouse for his nightly visit. As soon as he was inside they rushed up to the back of the outhouse, prepared to push it over again. They were laughing so hard that George certainly heard them, but he paid no attention.

By the time they discovered their mistake it was too late. George had moved the house three feet forward, and before they could stop, they plunged into the pit, up to their waists in what we might call human fertilizer.

The outhouse had been in use for many years, so the contents of the pit had ripened very well. It took several days for the boys to wash the smell from their bodies. They burned their clothes.

George Tobin was once again the "King of the Pranksters."

Chapter 5

INTO THE MILITARY – 1946

I had wanted to enlist in the Army at the end of my junior year of high school, but Dad insisted that I finish high school first. Dad had gone to school to about the fourth grade and he was determined that his son would get a better education. So, as soon as I graduated from East Chain High School, in June of 1946, I persuaded him to give me written permission to go into the service.

There were some good reasons that I wanted to go into the military; Mom's father was in the Spanish-American War, in Cuba, Dad was in during World War I, and my sister's husband was in Italy during World War II.

The whole country was on a patriotic kick, and I didn't want to be left behind.

Besides, there was no future for me on the farm and I was eager to get on with my life.

I contacted the Recruiting Office in Mankato, the nearest town that had a recruiting office, and volunteered to go into the Army. I received a letter telling me to report to the Recruiting Office, ready to go. I reported in and was sent, by bus, to Ft. Snelling, near St. Paul, Minnesota, where I filled out the necessary papers, and was given a physical examination. I was sworn into the Army Air Corps on June 28, 1946. It was my 18th birthday.

A few days later, a group of us recruits were placed on a train bound for San Antonio, Texas, via Oklahoma City, Oklahoma.

Before I discuss my military career, I'd like to mention the fact that the Air Force was a branch of the Army until August 1, 1947, therefore, in 1946, I came under Army regulations and wore an Army uniform. The Army Air Corps was a branch of the Army at the same level as the Corps of Engineers, the Medical Corps, or the Infantry. I had a choice as to which branch of the Army that I wanted, so I chose the Air Corps. It wasn't until 1949 that the Air Force began issuing the blue uniforms that are worn today.

Basic Training

When we pulled into the station in San Antonio, we were met by an Army bus and taken to the San Antonio Army Air Corps Cadet Center (later renamed Lackland Air Force Base), and we were herded into a two-story, 50-man barracks, which was to be our home for the next six weeks.

Basic training was quite an experience. I had never been subjected to such discipline and physical conditioning, but I had no trouble handling the training. My father had taught me about discipline and I was in good condition from being raised on the farm, so basic training wasn't too tough for me. There were times when I wanted to die, and other times I was so proud that I grinned all day.

****

In January 2013 my grandson, Andrew Monson, graduated from basic training at Lackland Air Force Base, 67 years after I was there. I put on my Air Force uniform and went to San Antonio for the graduation weekend. Strutting around the base in that uniform was a real blast. It's not too often that basic trainees, or their instructors, have a chance to meet an 84-year-old graduate of the training center, so many of them came up to me, introduced themselves, and wanted to talk. It was a great honor to be with these young airmen, and to learn about today's Air Force. While I was there I visited the new Air Force Airman's Museum being constructed at Lackland and gave them some information about my experiences there. I later completed a questionnaire and mailed them some photographs taken while I was in basic training. I suppose that my information is on file at the Museum.

The words "Airman" or "Airmen" are no longer gender sensitive. An airman is an airman and that's all there is to it. Some of us old-timers remember the WAFs, but that's history.

In many ways, basic training has changed a great deal from the time that I was there. They still have the same requirements for neatness of appearance, for discipline, for physical fitness and for close-order drill, but the graduation ceremony, with its personal recognition of outstanding airmen, and the grand parade that finalized the ceremony, was entirely new to me.

When I attended basic training, in 1946, as soon as we finished basic training, we were put on trains to go to our technical training schools. There was no final ceremony.

The most noticeable difference was that the training program is now managed by sergeants, whereas, in my time there was a Lieutenant involved in our day-to-day activities

Another bit of activity that has changed, is that we performed KP (kitchen police) and guard duty, about once a week, something that is now done by contract employees. KP was an old tradition in the military. Each flight was assigned, for about one day a week, to a specific mess hall, and we worked from 5:00 AM until 8:00 PM, with breaks only to eat, We did all of the duties in the mess hall, except the cooking, which was done by military enlisted personnel. As you can imagine, it was a very dirty and tiring task. KP was the most despised duty in basic training.

Guard duty was simply teaching us how to maintain security. The tour of duty was from dark until daylight, performed in two-hour shifts, with two hours of sleep time between shifts. The next day was a full day of normal activity. The weapon that we used for this duty was a .30 caliber carbine, without ammunition. We walked a post, which was assigned to us by the Corporal of the Guard, and any carelessness or error, would result in severe punishment.

Being back at Lackland AFB was a great experience.

****

We were all tested to determine our capabilities and were given assignments to technical schools. I was selected to receive radar training in Florida.

How we were selected for training was quite interesting. A couple hundred of us were placed in a meeting hall full of school-type desks. We began taking proficiency tests around 8:00 AM and continue taking tests until after 6:00 PM. Each test was progressively more difficult than the one before it and as each was finished and graded, there were fewer men in the room. When we finished, that night, only 12 men remained in the room. All 12 of us went to radar school at Boca Raton Army Air Field, Florida.

So off to radar school I went. We were loaded onto a World War II troop train, and about a week later, we arrived in Boca Raton, Florida. That was not an enjoyable trip. The train had the lowest priority on the rail line, so we were forced onto the siding by every passenger and freight train that came along. There were no bunks on the train, so we slept, sitting up, on straight-backed, bench type seats.

Following is a story about basic training.

Real Men
San Antonio, Texas – 1946

Early in Army Air Corps basic training, our lieutenant led us on a 5-mile hike on open country roads and, somewhere in the first few miles, he missed a turn in the road, and we walked 21 miles.

As we walked along we weren't aware of how far we had gone, but later that day, the lieutenant went back, in his car, and measured the distance that we had walked. He was a good officer and he came into the barracks that night and told us of the error and apologized for it. I think that our respect for him went up a lot that night. By the way, he was walking in dress shoes, and we were in combat boots.

We had two guys in that flight that I remember quite well. One was "Happy" Bowman, 6'3" and about 220 pounds. The other was

"Shorty" Lego, barely 5 feet tall and, maybe 100 pounds. Midway through the hike, Shorty developed blisters on both feet. There was blood in his boots but he wouldn't quit. Without saying a word, Happy picked him up, placed him on his shoulders, and carried him the rest of the way.

Basic training produces real men, large and small.

In the last week of training, our Flight entered Close-Order-Drill Competitions for the entire basic training center.

We won the competition.

We received a great deal of praise for winning and our commanding officer gave us extra passes to town.

The final activity of basic training was a three-day trip to Camp Bullock, for bivouac, designed to acquaint us with conditions in the field. We carried our own 2-man pup-tents, and dug our own slit-trench latrines. We took 10-mile, late-night hikes, with full packs and one canteen of water per man. We ate out of tin cans (C-rations), fired M-30 carbines on the rifle range, and learned to live with nature. Some of the wild animals that lived with us were raccoons, armadillos, and rattlesnakes. I can still remember the sound of a man screaming, in the middle of the night, when he stubbed his toe on an armadillo, and thought it was a rattlesnake.

All of this was in late August, when daytime temperatures reached over 110 degrees.

Chapter 6

TECHNICAL SCHOOL

Boca Raton Army Air Field was a World War II base, located about halfway between Fort Lauderdale and Miami, Florida. When it was built most of the vegetation and the waterways were left in place and winding roads were carved out of the Everglades. Wherever there was some high ground, single-story, wooden, buildings were built, among the trees, and covered with camouflage tarpaper. The areas were connected by narrow, winding roads. During the war the base was totally camouflaged, complete with artificial trees that were placed on the runway when an air raid was anticipated.

There were no sidewalks.

A typical squadron area consisted of six, 40-man, barracks, a latrine building, a supply building, and an orderly room, which contained the offices of the squadron officers, the 1ˢᵗ Sgt, and the administrative staff. Surrounding each of these camouflaged areas was the swamp, with all of the native animals and vegetation. To get from one building to another, we walked among the trees, through the sand.

The mess halls were single-story, rambling, buildings with coal-fired cook stoves, which could feed about a hundred troops at each meal. They were open 24 hours a day, to accommodate students who attended classes in three, eight-hour, shifts, five days a week. I can well remember standing in block-long lines, in the middle of the night, waiting for a meal.

The first course in radar school was Radar Fundamentals, a 16-week course of basic electronics. Normally, when a class finished that phase, the men were assigned to advanced classes, depending upon the grades they received in the basic course

But, shortly after I got there, everything changed. When we finished fundamentals, we were told that there were very few openings in the advanced classes for any of us. Most of the troops, who didn't go to advanced classes, right away, followed a revolving schedule of KP and guard duty. They worked in the mess hall from 5:00 AM until 10:00 PM, then slept until late the next morning, loafed through the day, and then went on guard duty, somewhere in the swamp, from sundown to sunrise. After guard duty they slept all day and part of the night, and then went back on KP at 5:00 the next morning. For some people, this went on, seven days a week, for over four months.

During that time, many men went AWOL, and there were a few suicides.

No one seemed to care.

About a month before I completed Radar Fundamentals, our Barracks Chief finished school and moved on, so the 1st Sgt came to the barracks and asked if anyone would like to volunteer to be the new Barracks Chief. I don't know why I did it, but I volunteered for the job. I suppose that I figured that I could get some ego-building experience without doing much of anything. It didn't turn out that way.

The 1st Sgt called me to the Orderly Room and handed me orders that appointed me to the rank of Acting Corporal. That meant that I now had all of the responsibilities and privileges of a noncommissioned officer, but was still being paid as a Private. He told me to sew on my new stripes.

Consider this; I was 18 years old, had been in the Army for less than six months and I was now supervising the activities of 39 men, most of them older than I was.

What follows is a demonstration of how leadership skills were acquired in the "old Army."

A few weeks after I was named Barracks Chief, I was assigned to a different barracks. According to the 1st Sgt, the chief of that barracks had been relieved from duty because the place was a mess.

I moved to my new barracks, selected the first bunk inside of the door, and took charge. The first night, several of the men refused to turn off their radios when "lights out" was called. Without saying anything, I went to the main fuse box and pulled the circuit breaker. The next morning I went to the orderly room and canceled the liberty passes of every man in the barracks for one week

I thought that I had taught them a lesson, but apparently I hadn't. The next Friday afternoon I directed the men to scrub the floor in preparation for the Saturday morning inspection. They all remained sitting on their bunks, doing nothing.

A tall, slender, kid began spouting off about how I had no authority to tell him anything. I walked over to him and told him to stand up. When he didn't get up, I grabbed the front of his shirt and jerked him to his feet. We sparred for a few seconds, and then he lunged forward, threw his right arm around my neck, and tried to throw me to the floor. As his arm tightened around my neck, I looked up, and out of the corner of my eye I saw his chin, just above my head. I drove my right fist upward, as hard as I could, and hit him on the point of his chin. He released his grip and dropped to the floor. He didn't try to get up. I turned and walked to my bunk at the other end of the barracks. I sat down on my bunk and when I looked up I noticed that everyone had rapidly begun to scrub the floor.

I had no trouble with any of those men again. Within three weeks, we were named the "Barracks of the Week," and they were all given liberty passes to town for the weekend. All of a sudden, they seemed to accept me.

The way that I got the job done wouldn't be condoned in the military today. Back then, the noncoms got the job done, there was no record of the incident, and everybody found out about life in the real world. If a noncom in today's military struck someone, he would be in big trouble.

So you see, Old Sarge and Beetle Bailey really did exist, many years ago.

After about three months, I was transferred to another squadron and took a six-week course in Radar Mechanics - Altimeters.

I received orders to be assigned to the 7th Geodetic Control Squadron, at MacDill Field, Tampa, Florida.

Following are some stories about Boca Raton Field.

First Sergeant
Boca Raton Army Air Field, Florida – 1947

First Sergeant Montera had been in the infantry, during World War II, fighting his way from Australia to Japan without a scratch. He told me that the closest he'd come to being wounded was when, while he was crawling on his belly during a beach landing, a sniper had shot the heel off of his boot.

He was tough as nails, and one hell of a good First Shirt.

Less than 20 yards from our barracks area, was the base stockade, surrounded by a 15-foot-high, wire fence, patrolled by armed guards.

One morning about 3:00 AM, Sgt Montera, and the rest of us, was awakened by a guard, singing at the top of his lungs. We all laid quietly in our bunks, waited for him to explode.

He did.

"What in hell are you squallin' about?" Monty bellowed. He had gotten out of bed and gone to the window. His voice was loud and clear.

We all held our breath.

"I gotta have somethin' to do," was the meek reply.

By now, the night birds had stopped singing. The swamp animals had ceased calling. It was deathly quiet. They sensed that trouble was brewing.

"Stick your dick in your mouth, you stupid son-of-a-bitch," he screamed, "That'll give you something to do."

Apparently the guard had heard about 1ˢᵗ Sgt. Montera, and had recognized his voice, because the singing stopped.

The jungle sounds resumed and we all went back to sleep.

THE NURSES
Boca Raton Army Air Field, Florida – 1947

Sgt. Britt was our Duty Sergeant, the squadron enforcer. He was just a little guy, but tougher than a prairie bronco. He was God, and don't you ever forget it.

To understand this incident, you must remember that the base was very large, and that the barracks areas were scattered far and wide. We seldom saw anyone that we didn't know.

Most Saturday afternoons we lounged around the barracks area, or soaked up the sun in the sandy yard, wearing as little clothing as we could get away with.

On one such Saturday, one of the men decided to create a little amusement, so he blew up a condom to about 2 feet in diameter and tossed it into the air.

A gust of wind carried the balloon about 20 feet into the air, toward the street, just as a little red convertible came cruising around the curve in the street.

Riding in the convertible were three very young and very happy Army nurses. The balloon floated in the air for a few seconds and then landed, smack dab, in the front seat of the car.

Now, if that had happened today, the girls probably would have stopped to locate the guy who owned a condom of that size, but this was 1946, and condoms were not items of proper conversation.

The nurses giggled, batted the balloon out of the car, and sped away, waving happily as they went. We cheered them on as they left.

That should have been the end of it, but it wasn't. Sgt. Britt had observed the whole episode. He came charging out of the orderly room and nailed the poor, unfortunate owner of the condom. Later that night, the soldier was observed burying the condom in a 6 x 6 x 6 foot hole in the sand, using a 4 x 4 inch trenching tool.

No one dared to laugh.

Chapter 7

FIRST PERMANENT ASSIGNMENT

About a half-dozen of us graduates walked into the radar shack, on the flight-line, ready to go to work. SSgt Munson T. Daly, the Noncommissioned Officer in Charge (NCOIC) of the radar repair unit, greeted us and asked if any one of us knew how to type. Since I had taken typing in high school, I raised my hand. He told me to sit down while he assigned the other men to their duties.

As it turned out, I never did do any radar work. I stayed in Sgt Daly's office, maintaining his file of radar manuals, and typing his correspondence, until I was given a hardship discharge in May of 1948. It was a relatively easy job. I kept the manuals up to date, typed correspondence, and did anything else that Sgt. Daly told me to do. I managed to keep my nose out of other people's business, did my job, and five months later, I was promoted to Corporal (Cpl). A couple of months after that, I met the board for promotion to Sergeant, but because I couldn't answer technical questions correctly, I didn't get promoted.

In January of 1948, my parents moved to New Rockford, North Dakota to take over the operation of a 400 acre dairy farm. Dad came down with pneumonia shortly after they got there, and they asked me to get out of the Army to come home and help them. I received a hardship discharge on May 11th.

What happened here is a good example of what can happen to someone who doesn't plan ahead.

After I got discharged, I worked on the farm in North Dakota for about four months, then bummed around the country for a while, and went back into the Air Force on September 15, 1949. Chapter 8 tells about my adventures during those 17 months of civilian life. It was a period of adventure and makes for pretty good reading, but it was a time of no upward movement in my life.

I had learned electronics in technical school, but never used the skills during my military career. I spent most of my 20 years in the Air Force in administrative positions and was promoted on schedule for six years, to the rank of Technical Sergeant. Then, after the Korean War was over and the armed forces were reduced in size, many of the hi-tech people left the service, for higher paying jobs, but because there were very few jobs on the outside, for my skills, I stayed in. Within my career field there were very few promotions, at my level, for nearly 12 years. I was finally promoted to Master Sergeant, during the Vietnam War, just two years before I retired.

During the last 7 years of my military service I attended a technical college, taking classes at night, and I graduated with a degree in Electronic Engineering Technology, two weeks after I retired from the Air Force. I worked in the electronics industry for 20 years, and retired again at the age of 59. My first paycheck in my first civilian job was nearly triple the size of the last one that I received in the military.

How would my life have been different if I had stayed in electronics in 1947? I would have very likely been promoted to Master Sergeant about 10 years sooner than I was, or I could have gotten out earlier and taken advantage of the big bucks.

****

Before we leave the MacDill story, I'd like to tell you a little about what I did in my leisure time while I was assigned there.

Soon after I got to Tampa, I discovered a roller-skating rink on Davis Island, not far from downtown. I went there nearly every Saturday night, for most of the time that I was at MacDill.

There were many high school girls who skated at that rink, and I got to know several of them. There is no need for me to talk about the beautiful Cuban girls, because I met someone who took a small chunk out of my life. Her name was Judy, a 16-year-old high school kid, who was very attractive and quite popular with the guys.

It wasn't long, before we were together most of the time and I fell in love. She was an orphan girl, who lived with her Aunt. Her Aunt was a nice lady and she drove us around on weekends, so that I could see the Tampa area. Judy and I went to quite a few movies, went swimming at a local pool, and just hung out together.

When I learned that I was going to be discharged, I just couldn't bear to be away from her, so I asked her to marry me. She said "Yes" and I gave her a $100 diamond ring.

When I got discharged, I got a room in a cheap hotel near where Judy lived, spent a couple of days with her, and then I walked to the highway, stuck out my thumb and headed for Nebraska, where my sister, Virginia, lived.

I left Tampa on Saturday and arrived in Oshkosh, Nebraska on Tuesday, having traveled nearly 2000 miles in three days, with no sleep and very little food. When I got there, a letter from Mom was waiting, telling me that, because Dad was still too weak to work, I needed to hurry home as soon as possible. The next day I was on a Greyhound bus, bound for North Dakota.

Chapter 8

WORKING AND WANDERING

Near New Rockford, North Dakota, we were operating a 400-acre dairy farm, with all of the hard work that went with it. The only break in the routine was on Sunday, when we usually didn't do field work, but still milked the cows, fed the livestock, and cleaned the barn.

My job, in addition to the morning and evening chores, was that of a field hand. Most days I was on a tractor, doing whatever we were doing at the time. In the spring we plowed, disked and dragged the fields and planted the seed for three crops; wheat, oats and corn.

During the summer we cultivated the corn and mowed, raked, and baled hay. In late August we harvested the wheat and the oats, but most of the summer, we baled hay.

Since we had over 30 cows, we needed a lot of hay to get through the winter, so Dad arranged for us to help bale about 500 acres of virgin prairie at a farm about 5 miles away. The haying crew worked from early morning to nearly dark, six days a week, for over six weeks. We received a percentage of the bales in exchange for our labor.

About three weeks after I got to North Dakota I received a letter from my Florida girlfriend, telling me that she no longer loved me and that our engagement was off. The news hit me like a rock. I had planned to work long enough to save a few bucks, then go to Florida and get married. I got drunk for a couple of Saturday nights, and then I went on with my life.

The haying crew consisted of six men, four from the owner's farm, plus Dad and me.

Every day, working two days ahead of the baling crew, a man mowed the prairie grass and, after it dried for a day, raked it into windrows, ready for baling. Each morning, as soon as the dew was off the grass, the baler followed the windrows, picked up the hay and produced bales, each about 4 feet long, and weighing about 50 pounds. On a flat-bed trailer/rack, hitched to the back of the baler, was one of the hired men, taking the bales as they came off the baler, and stacking them on the rack. When the rack was loaded, the baler stopped, the rack was unhitched, and an empty rack took its place.

As each rack was unhitched from the baler, I drove up, on my tractor, pulling an empty rack, which was connected to the baler. I then took the loaded rack to the haystack that Dad was building and threw the bales onto the stack, where he put them in place to make a nice, rectangular stack. As the stack got taller, the work got harder. Sometimes I had to throw the bales several feet above my head to reach the level of the top of the stack. As soon as I got the rack unloaded, I drove back to the baler, dropped off my empty rack and picked up another full load, thus completing the loop. This went on for about seven hours a day, six days a week. Each morning, before we went haying, and each night after we quit, we were at home, milking the cows and doing other chores.

The only day that we didn't work was Sunday and, since that was a day off, Saturday night was a night to unwind. Mr. Halverson, one of the hired hands on the haying crew, invited me to come to a saloon in the little town of Sheyenne, about seven miles from where we lived, to meet his three sons, and to have a few drinks. When I walked into the saloon Mr. Halverson introduced me to his oldest son, Bud, a 6-foot tall cowboy. Then he nodded toward the end of the bar, where a very pregnant woman was standing and said, "That's Bud's wife, she's about to pop, but she's in here every week." When I came in the following week, Bud told me that his wife had presented him with a son on Thursday, but she would be back the next week. And she was. Need I say more about the tough Western women?

After that first night, I was in that saloon every Saturday night all summer.

Many Sundays I drove to the Fort Totten Indian Reservation, near Devils Lake. The Reservation had some picnic grounds, a lake for fishing, and a roller-skating rink. They also had a rodeo every Sunday afternoon. The Indians ran the Rodeo, but the cowboys were local farm boys like me.

The first Sunday that I went, I watched the activities and decided that I could ride those saddle broncs as well as anybody. The guy at the signup table asked me for my name, but I didn't know anyone in the place, so I just grabbed a name out of the air and gave it to the guy. In those days I smoked a pipe most of the time and I had it lit-up at the rodeo. Some cowboys had called me "Smokey" just a few minutes before, so I decided to use "Smokey" as my first name. For a last name, I picked my Dad's family name, "Carlson," his name in Sweden and for the first few years he lived in America. So in Devils Lake, North Dakota, during the activities at the Indian reservation, I was "Smokey Carlson."

I used that alias for many years, whenever I didn't want my real name known,

We worked on that farm all summer and after all was settled we had about $1500 to show for a year's work. We quit and moved back to East Chain, Minnesota.

Mom and Dad moved into a little, rented, farmhouse and found jobs.

I wandered away.

Following are some stories about what I did for the next 10 months.

Jack's Place
Southern Minnesota – 1948

Jack had an 80 acre farm about a mile east of the village of East Chain, and in November, 1948, he hired me as a farm hand to drive his corn picker for about a month. There are only a couple things about that job that are worth mentioning.

One day the corn picker became jammed with corn stalks. I got off of the tractor to clear the blockage, but I made a very serious mistake; I failed to turn off the drive shaft that operated the picker, so the snapper rollers were still turning. The snapper rollers are the pair of five-foot long, grooved rollers that strip the corn ears from the corn stalks.

When I started to pull the jammed corn stalks from between the rollers, the fingertip of one of my gloves got caught by the rollers. I jerked my hand back, and fortunately, the glove slipped off of my hand. The glove went through the rollers and landed on the ground under the picker. I looked down, expecting to see a bloody mess, but all of my fingers were still there. The good Lord must have been looking out for idiots that day, because I knew several men who had lost an arm, or had bled to death, while doing the same fool thing that I had just done.

****

I must tell you that Jack was not a very industrious farmer. Most of the farmers raised several litters of pigs each year, feeding them until they weighed a hundred pounds or more, and then selling them to a slaughterhouse. One of the necessary tasks that the farmers performed was that of castrating all of the male pigs when they were just a few weeks old. The farmers knew that if they didn't do that, after a few months, those little boy pigs would begin to get grown-up ideas about the little girl pigs.

Well, Jack hadn't bothered to complete that task and his male pigs had gotten to be big healthy boys. Some of Jack's wayward boy pigs had jumped the fences and were playing with some of the girl pigs across the road. The neighbor was quite upset, because he didn't like the idea that some of Jack's naughty boys were fathering little bastards within his purebred herd.

So, one rainy day, when weather conditions prevented us from picking corn, he decided that we had time to castrate his pigs. Jack felt that we probably needed some help in that very tiring job, so he went to the house and got a bottle of whiskey. While he was doing that, I picked up a 2-gallon pail and filled it with cold water. Now, totally prepared for the task at hand, we went into the pig yard, corralled all the males, and drove them into a stall in the barn.

Jack placed the bottle of whiskey on a shelf, I put the pail of water on the floor, and we were ready to go to work. I grabbed a pig by a hind leg, threw him to the floor on his side, and put my knee on his neck to hold him down. Then I pulled his leg forward so Jack could do his surgical procedure. As Jack cut out each testicle, he tossed it into the pail of cold water. Then he reached over, took down the bottle of whisky, took a long swig, and handed the bottle to me. I let go of the pig, took a gulp from the bottle, and put it back on the shelf. The pig walked away, a bit humped over, with a pained expression on his face.

We repeated the cycle 22 times before we were finished.

When we got done, we threw away the empty whiskey bottle, took the pail to the house, washed our hands, Jack fried the testicles and we ate them for dinner. My memory of that day is a bit fuzzy, but I think we enjoyed the meal.

Wandering
United States – 1948-49

In the fall of 1948, after the corn harvest was completed, I decided to go back to Tampa, Florida, to visit my old haunts. I packed up my Army backpack, picked up my roller skates case, and headed for Florida on a Greyhound bus.

When I arrived in Tampa, with about $150 in my pocket, I started walking around the edge of downtown to find a place to stay. I found an old house that was displaying a "Rooms for Rent" sign, went in, and rented a room for two weeks.

That night, carrying my roller skates, I went out to the skating rink where I had skated for over a year, when I was stationed at MacDill

Field. I expected to find some of my friends, and sure enough, they were there. Also there was Judy, the girl that I had proposed to, just a few months earlier.

I went over to where she was sitting, stopped in front of her, and said, "I've come to get my ring back." She looked up, sort of startled, and began to laugh. I won't go into the details of what she said, except that she had hocked the ring about a week after I left town. I left the roller rink and went back to my rented room.

I spent a week alternating between getting drunk and looking for work, without have much success in either endeavor.

When my money began to run out, I decided to go west to Texas, find work on a ranch until the next summer, and then work my way north on a wheat threshing crew. Dad had told me about working the harvest from Texas to Canada, during his younger years, and I thought it might be fun to try it. As I prepared to pack up and leave, I began to think about my safety while hitchhiking across the country. I had hitchhiked many times before without fear, but for some reason I felt that I needed some type of protection. I went to a pawnshop and traded my roller skates for a .32 caliber H&R revolver and a box of shells.

The next morning I packed my backpack and prepared to leave Tampa. Before I left the room, I put the gun shells in my pack, and shoved the pistol into the inside of my right boot. Now I felt safe enough to travel. I checked out from my room, walked to the north side of Tampa, found a wide intersection on US Highway 41, and stuck out my thumb.

By midafternoon I had caught several rides and walked many miles, taking me up Highway 41, nearly to the Georgia line. At one point, because the gun was wearing a blister on my leg, I took it from my boot and put it into my backpack.

A few minutes later, a car stopped and the driver asked me where I was going. I told him that I was going to Texas to find work. He said that he was going as far as Houston and to jump in. We proceeded north, then west, across the Florida Panhandle.

About midnight, we reached the town of Slidell, Louisiana, and he told me that he was going to stop for the night.

I got out, and because I was pretty tired, I started to look for a place to curl up for the night. As I walked down the street I came upon an abandoned service station. It seemed to me that the building would provide a place for me to sleep and in the morning I would get something to eat and head on down the road. The first door that I checked was unlocked, so I decided to go in.

Just as I started to open the door a car, with a flashing red light on the top, screeched to a stop, right next to me. A short, fat, man wearing khakis and a cowboy hat and totin' a tied-down revolver on his hip, jumped out. He demanded to know what I was doing in his town. It turned out that he was the town marshal, and he had seen me breaking into a building. I thought that I might have a problem.

He shouted at me, "Keep your hands where I can see 'em, and hand me your pack." I gave him the pack, and stood real still. He began rummaging through the pack, and down in the bottom, he found the box of shells. He got very excited. In fact, he was so excited that he could hardly talk. He quickly rummaged through the rest of the pack and finally found the pistol. He pushed me against his car, and cuffed my hands behind my back. I asked him why I had been arrested, and he said, "Dangerous and suspicious." I nearly laughed. Me? Dangerous and suspicious? Ridiculous. Anyway, he took me to the local lockup, put me in a cell, and went away. I reasoned that, at least, I now had a place to sleep. The cell was clean, and the cot looked comfortable, so I laid down and went to sleep.

The next morning about 8:00 o'clock, a deputy sheriff came and took me to Covington, where the Sheriff's office and the county jail were located. On the ride over, which took about 20 minutes, the deputy and I got acquainted. He was a nice guy, not much older than I was. He told me that he had noticed my military papers in my backpack, and that he was a veteran too. He told me that since I was armed I had to be considered dangerous, but since the gun was in my pack and not on my person, I hadn't been charged with anything. He felt that, after the three-day confinement limit, on people who weren't being charged, I probably would be released.

He put me in a cell and asked me if I was hungry. I told him that I hadn't had any food in over 24 hours, and that I could us some. He sent in the jailer with a plate of food that didn't look very promising. I had a few dollars left in my pocket, so I handed the jailer some money and asked him to go across the street to a diner and get me some breakfast. He looked at me kind of funny, but he went and got me my breakfast. Then he sat down and we talked while I was eating. He chuckled when he said that I was the first prisoner that he had ever had who sent out for his meals.

On the afternoon of the third day the jailer opened the door and took me to the sheriff's office. The sheriff told me that there had been some gas station robberies, by a man of my description, but when they checked out my story, they knew that I wasn't the man they were looking for and that I was free to go.

I found a cheap hotel and got a room. I didn't ask him about the gun.

It felt good to be free again.

I went downstairs to a small bar and when I walked in I noticed that one of the men sitting at the bar was the same deputy who had brought me from Slidell to Covington. He bought me a beer, we talked for an hour or so, and he wished me good luck in my travels.

The next morning I had a long talk with myself, during which I decided that I probably would be better off farther north. So I walked to the Greyhound bus station, gave all my money to the clerk, and asked him how far north I could get on that money. He calculated for a bit and told me that I could get a ticket to Kansas City.

Later in the day I boarded the bus and rode for about a day and a half, and got off in Kansas City.

It was getting dark and it was cold and raining. I took my pack and started to walk towards the edge of town.

A man picked me up, as I walked along the street, and asked me where I was going. I told him that I was headed for my home in Minnesota but that I had absolutely no money and I was hungry. He gave me two dollars, and wished me well as I got out of the car. I went to the nearest diner and spent the money on a couple of bowls of chili. It warmed me up and lifted my spirits.

It was about eight o'clock at night when I was on the road again, and as I traveled north the rain turned to snow, the wind came up, and the temperature began to drop.

About two in the morning, I was dropped off at the intersection of a road that led to Garner, Iowa, about a half-mile away. A blizzard was raging and traffic had nearly stopped. I stood by the side of the road for over three hours, dressed only in my old khaki uniform and a light jacket. I had no gloves and my boots were frozen stiff. I began to grow sleepy and I wanted to lie down and go to sleep. My body began to feel nice and warm.

I knew that I was freezing to death.

I started walking toward the town, hoping that I could find some shelter. When I arrived in town, I discovered that the railroad station was open and the station agent had just built a fire in preparation for the seven o'clock train. I dropped onto a bench and fell asleep. I was awakened by a highway patrolman who asked me some very pointed questions about where I had been and where I was going. He apparently was satisfied with my answers because he went away and left me alone.

After daylight, I walked back to the main road, and caught a ride north. The blizzard had stopped, but the temperature was about 20° and the roads were covered with packed snow and ice. I managed to get good rides to Albert Lea, Minnesota, where I headed west on Highway 16.

Just west of Albert Lee, I was picked up by a drunken man with a wife and a baby in the car. He drove like a maniac on the frozen roads, and to top it all, his brother and family were in another car, just ahead of us. He also was drunk. At one point the guy that I was with decided to pass his brother, and as we came abreast of the other car, his brother apparently panicked and spun the steering wheel, causing the car to slide sideways, into the ditch, in a cloud of snow. Luckily, he didn't roll. We stopped, helped him put on his tire chains, and then I drove the car out of the ditch for him. The incident apparently sobered the brothers some, because they drove more sensibly the rest of the way to Fairmont. In Fairmont, I chanced upon someone from Each Chain, who gave me a lift home.

It was the Saturday before Christmas and my parents were glad to see me; they hadn't heard from me in over two months. I filled them in on the details and settled in. I was home again.

Moving on

I spent the holidays with my parents, and then began looking for a job. I was in the employment office in Fairmont in mid-January 1949, when a man came in who was looking for a farmhand to work on a dairy farm near Beloit, Wisconsin. We talked for a few minutes and I accepted the job, on the condition that I could report for work after February 2nd, my parent's 25th wedding anniversary.

On February 4, 1949, I arrived at Swiss Town Farms, about two miles north of Beloit.

The farm was a large dairy operation, owned by the A.O. Smith Corporation of Milwaukee and used as an experimental farm for their newly invented, fiberglass-coated, blue, "Harvestore" silos, that now can be seen all over the country.

I found that it was a very interesting place to work, with some very nice people. The work crew consisted of the farm manager, who was a young man just out of college, a herdsman, and two laborers, one of which was me. Part of my pay was free room and board and I was to live with the herdsman and his family. Their house was a four bedroom, typical Midwestern, farmhouse with nice furnishings and plenty of living space. It was quite comfortable.

And so I went to work on the farm. The dairy herd consisted of about 75 Brown Swiss cows, with about 40 of them producing milk at any given time.

We worked hard on the dairy farm, seven days a week, from 5:00 in the morning to 8:00 at night. We milked 40 cows, twice a day, fed the livestock, and cleaned the barn.

I really liked working on that farm. The crew was good to work with, I was making a decent wage, and I was quite content in what I was doing. I worked seven days a week, but did manage to have some fun every Saturday night, when I went roller skating at the National Guard Armory, in Beloit.

But that was not to last very long.

I had been there for about two months when, one night, I was awakened when I felt the presence of someone sitting on the edge of my bed. I looked up, to see the herdsman's wife looking down at me. She wanted to talk. She told me a sad story about how her husband had gotten her pregnant when she was sixteen years old and that she now wanted to leave him and their two sons and go away with me. I knew I had a problem. She sobbed for a while, and then left the room.

I worked through the next day, had supper with them, and then went to bed. After midnight, I got up, packed my backpack, and slipped out the door. I went to the barn, where there was a phone, and called a Beloit taxi.

I moved into the cheapest hotel in Beloit, and went to work as the floor manager of a roller skating rink.

One morning, about a month and a half later, I picked up the Beloit newspaper, and noticed an ad from the Industrial Training Institute, in Chicago, that said the school was looking for students, and that a representative would be at a hotel in Beloit that evening. I met with the man and found out that they were a training school, teaching refrigeration and air-conditioning repair. I also learned that they were certified to accept students who were World War II veterans and qualified for the G.I. Bill of Rights. Two days later, I was in Chicago.

Chicago

I took the elevated (L) train to the school, located at 2400 Lawrence Ave, on the Chicago North Side, and registered for classes. The registration office found a room for me at a rooming house about two blocks from the school, and I moved in. As an unmarried veteran, the GI Bill would pay for all of my school costs, complete with books and school supplies, plus $75 a month. I paid about $40 a month for my room, leaving me $35 to live on, so I knew that I had to find a job.

For a couple of weeks, I worked after school at odd jobs in the neighborhood, but the nation was going through an economic recession, and jobs were scarce.

I discovered that Wilson & Company was hiring at their meatpacking plant on the South Side. I lived at 4700 North Winchester Ave. and the packing plant was at 40th Street, South. That's 87 blocks by elevated train. I landed a job with Wilson and began working from 9:00 PM to 6:00 AM, loading meat onto city delivery trucks.

The loading dock crew consisted of four teams, each with a checker (the guy with the invoices on a clipboard), and four very strong men, who loaded the trucks. The loaders were mostly guys who would rather fight than work. Before I started working there, I thought that I was tough, but compared to them, I was a pussycat. Hardly a week went by that there wasn't at least one fight, sometimes with knives or meat hooks. Fortunately for everybody, our foreman, Mister Wiley was an old man about 70 and could break up fights just by yelling at the men involved. They somehow respected the old cuss, even though they knew that they could kill him without thinking about it.

Now let's look at my situation. I went to school from 9:00 AM to 2:00 PM each day and I left my room for work at 8:00 PM and returned to my room about 7:00 AM. That left me with two hours in the morning and six hours in the afternoon, to eat, sleep, and do homework. My grades began to slip from straight A's to nearly failing.

I lasted until mid-September.

One morning I woke up, opened one eye, and said to myself, "to hell with it," rolled over and went back to sleep. About noon, I got up, went to the Air Force recruiting office, and reenlisted.

Since I had been trained in radar maintenance, a critical career field, they had a big need for me back in the Air Force. But, since I knew very few people in Chicago, I couldn't come up with the three letters of character reference and three letters of credit reference that were required for my reenlistment. The recruiting sergeant told me, "Come back tomorrow, I'll see what I can do about the references." Sure enough, the next afternoon, he had six letters, all signed by local merchants, who said what a nice and honest fellow I was. Three days later, I was on a train, headed for refresher training at Lackland Air Force Base, San Antonio, Texas.

I worked at the plant that night, as usual, then waited around for the Plant Superintendent, to tell him that I was quitting. When he heard what I was going to do, he began to swear. He told me that he had intended to promote me to be the Foreman of the night loading dock crew, to replace Old Man Wiley, who was going to retire. Since I had already signed the papers to go back in the Air Force, I couldn't consider the job, but I have often wondered what would have happened if I had taken that foreman's job. I might have been stabbed to death the first week, or maybe I would have become president of the company. No one will ever know.

At this point, I was 21 years old and still didn't know what I wanted to do with my life. As I look back at that period, I now realize that I had picked up a great deal of experience that helped me to succeed in my later years. I wasn't aware of it at the time, but I had worked for over three years as an adult, usually being trusted to do difficult jobs, with very little supervision, and that

I had matured into a man without realizing what had happened. During those 17 months, I had some interesting adventures, without making much money, but I was gaining a lot of experience along the way..

Chapter 9

WIESBADEN, GERMANY – 1949-52

After several weeks of refresher training in San Antonio, I was assigned to Wiesbaden Air Base, Germany. Travel was by train to New York, troopship to Bremerhaven, Germany, then by train to Wiesbaden, arriving on Dec 6, 1949.

When I got to Wiesbaden Air Base, it was discovered that the Air Force had intended to send me to a radar repair facility in southern Germany, but had goofed up my orders. While the personnel office was trying to straighten things out, they put me to work in the Base Headquarters Mail Room.

They eventually reclassified me to Clerk Typist and I went on with my life.

On the first of March, I was sent on Temporary Duty (TDY) to Headquarters, European Command, in Heidelberg, to participate in joint maneuvers with the Army. I was there for six weeks and I had a ball.

I landed a job as a clerk, working for the Operations Historical Officer, a nice, motherly, WAF Major. She liked me and let me do about anything that I wanted to do, as long as I did her clerical work properly.

Nearly every night I went to town, and drank beer at the Red Ox, the famous beer Keller near Heidelberg University. The young German students spoke English fluently, and they all had money, so we had a good time. Those fellows really knew how to drink. On one occasion a young man downed all of the beer from a one-foot-tall glass mug, shaped like a woman's boot, without taking a breath. A few minutes after he finished the beer, someone handed him the same boot, filled with wine, and he drank that too. When I left, about 11:00 o'clock, that young man was still on his feet, dancing with the ladies.

After six weeks, I came back from Heidelberg, only to find that I had been reassigned to the Personnel Office, in the same building that I had been in when I left.

Her name was *Ursula Maus*, a tall, slender, blond, German woman, who was a clerk typist in the Personnel Office. When I had worked in the mailroom, she was the one who picked up the mail for the Personnel Office and I had tried to get acquainted with her, but she wasn't interested. When I began working in the same office where she was, she couldn't avoid me, and we got to know each other a little better. In December 1950, Ursula became ill and was out of work for over two weeks. One afternoon, Staff Sgt. Canter, our boss, asked me if I would like to go with him to see Ursula at her home, and I reluctantly agreed.

Ursula's illness was quite unique. In 1945, right after the war ended, 17-year-old Ursula had worked in a department store as a sales clerk. The building had no heat, because there was no fuel-oil available, and she got frostbite on her thighs, between the tops of her stockings and her underwear. Now, five years later, the skin had gotten dry and cracked open, leaving nasty sores. The sores healed after a month or so, but she was very miserable for a while.

On February 12, 1951, I asked her for a date and she accepted. Since I didn't have a car, we agreed to meet on a certain street corner downtown. After work that day, I took the city bus into town, and walked to the corner where I thought I was supposed to meet her. I waited until 15 minutes past the appointed hour then, assuming that I had been "stood up," I headed toward the bus stop. I had gone about half a block when I heard someone calling my name. I turned around and there was Ursula, running toward me. I had been at the wrong corner, one block away from where I was supposed to be.

We had dinner at a nice restaurant, and went to a movie. Since I was "an American big spender" I ordered champagne with our meal.

That nice evening started a relationship that lasted for 42 years.

On March 4, 1951, we became engaged, but we couldn't get married right away. There were US military regulations that prohibited an American GI from marrying a German woman, until three months before he was scheduled to return to the States. The basic reason for this rule was that the authorities, both American and German, didn't want German nationals to have the same privileges as the families of the American troops. Remember, this was only four years after the war ended, and we Americans were an Army of Occupation.

I got to know her family and even though neither I, nor any of them, could speak the other's language, we somehow communicated very well. I had found a new home, with a new family to love.

Shortly after we became engaged I bought a black, 1948, 4-door Chevrolet, from my boss, Capt. Taylor. It was in excellent condition and he allowed me to pay him in monthly installments. I think I paid him about $850 for it. That car was my "courting car" until I sold it when we left Germany in November 1952.

During the rest of my time in Germany, we worked in the same building, and during our off-duty time, we were either at her home, or were enjoying ourselves somewhere in Europe. We went to movies, ice shows, music concerts and took cruises on the Rhine River. We traveled to many parts of Germany and took vacation trips to Luxembourg, Belgium, Holland, the German Alps, Switzerland, and Italy.

Along the way I was promoted, one step at a time, to Staff Sergeant.

On August 2, 1952, Ursula and I were married twice on the same day because the law in Germany recognized only civil ceremonies and we wanted to have a formal church wedding.

At 10 o'clock in the morning, we went to the Mayor's office, where the vows were read to us in German.

Whenever I was expected to reply, Ursula nudged me and I nodded my head and said, "I do."

Then, at 3 o'clock in the afternoon, we had a formal wedding, conducted by an Air Force Chaplain, in the American Church in downtown Wiesbaden.

After the church wedding, we had a reception at Ursula's home. Most of her family was there, along with eight of my military friends. Ursula's parents didn't have a very large apartment, but we set up their large table in the living/dining room, loaded it with cakes and other goodies, some wine, and had a wonderful day.

I took a three-day pass and we went to Brussels, Belgium, on our honeymoon. We didn't do much sightseeing while there, but it didn't really matter, because we were so interested in each other that we probably wouldn't have seen anything anyway.

Then we began the long hassle to obtain a US entry visa for Ursula. We went to the American Consulate in Frankfurt, filled out the papers, and went home to wait for her visa to arrive. I won't go into the details about our problems with the people at the Consulate, but the visa came in the mail less than a week before we were scheduled to depart.

I received my orders for assignment to Fort Snelling, Minnesota, so we reported to the passenger terminal at Rhine-Main Air Base early the morning of November 13, 1952, and flew out later that day aboard on an Air Force C-54.

Early the next morning we landed in Washington, DC.

That day was a very big day for Ursula. What more could anyone ask for, when coming to live in America, than to have your first step on the ground to be in the nation's capital.

The first order of business was to get an automobile. I had sold my Chevrolet in Germany, so we needed some wheels. As soon as we got to town we took a taxi to a used car lot and bought a 1949 Hudson 4-door sedan. Then we went sightseeing.

The next morning we headed west to visit my family. First we went to Fairmont, Minnesota to visit my parents and then, with Mom and Dad with us, we went to Nebraska to spend Christmas with my sister, Virginia, and her family. Then we drove back to Fairmont, and Ursula stayed with my folks while I went to St. Paul to find a place for us to live.

One of the most remarkable things about my family is the way that they accepted Ursula. They treated her as if they had known her all of her life. From that point on, she was a member of the Monson family. I was very proud of all of them.

Following is a description of Ursula's family, followed by some stories about Europe.

Maus Family
Wiesbaden, Germany – 1949-52

Before we go any further with this story, let's take a look at the family that I had joined.

Georg Christian Maus was born in Wiesbaden, Germany on December 4, 1896. He had siblings, but I don't know anything about them.

Frieda Johannette Ninna Maus was born in Wiesbaden, Germany on April 7, 1895. I met one of her sisters, Martha, a very jovial and likable person.

Georg and Frieda were married on August 28, 1920 in Wiesbaden, Germany. Most of their married life they lived at 2 Teutonenstrasse, Wiesbaden. Georg died in 1966 and Frieda died in 1980.

Georg and Frieda had four daughters: **Martha**, Marie-Louise **(Ria)**, **Lydia**, and **Ursula.**

I will try to reconstruct the family history, in a time sequence, for each of the four girls and their families.

Martha was married to a German soldier and they had one daughter, **Ingrid** in 1943. Martha's husband was captured by the

British and was held by them until 1948. After he returned from prison camp, he went to work in a large chemical plant. In the summer of 1949, a massive explosion at the plant killed over three hundred people, including him. Martha moved back in with her parents, bringing their daughter, **Ingrid,** with her.

In about 1950, she married Heinz Klitz, and they moved to Luxembourg. Heinz wouldn't take Ingrid, so Grandma Frieda raised her. Martha and Heinz had three sons, **Manfred**, **Walter**, and **Werner**, all born in Luxembourg. Heinz died many years ago. Martha had a stroke in 1992 and lived in a nursing home until she died in 1995.

Ingrid was born October 3, 1943 and lived at 2 Teutonenstrasse until she was old enough to go out on her own. She married Walter Edling, and had two daughters. She currently lives in Schlangenbad, not far from Wiesbaden.

Manfred is married and has a daughter. He lives in Luxembourg.

Walter is married and lives in Bonn, when not on work assignments outside of Germany.

Werner is married and has 2 daughters and a son. He has worked for the German State Department as a Foreign Service officer for many years. He has served in German embassies in various parts of the world.

Ria was working on Wiesbaden Air Base as the Base Commander's secretary in 1942 when she fell in love with the Base Commander's chauffeur. He was transferred to Italy, where he was killed when a truck crushed him against a loading dock. Their son, *Hans* was born on August 11, 1943. On March 20, 1949 Ria had a second son, *Wolfgang.* Ria, Hans, and Wolfgang all lived with the Maus family at 2 Teutonenstrasse, when I was in Germany. Ria had a stroke in 1993 and died a few years later.

Hans and his wife Marion had one son, Alexander, who died of leukemia at the age of nine. Hans has worked most of his adult life for the same firm, a large factory in Wiesbaden. He became very active in the labor movement and became head of the local union at the plant many years ago. As the top union official, he sat on the board of directors of the company. He became the local head of his political party, and as such became Vice-Mayor of Wiesbaden. He also served several years, in the State Legislature.

Wolfgang and Angelika were married on June 24, 1989, in Wiesbaden. Ursula and I flew to Germany for their wedding. They have two children, *__Julia__*, born July 19, 1992, and *__Maximillian__* (Max), born November 13, 1993. Wolfgang worked for a German phone company for a few years, and then started up his own company. He is now retired. I have kept in touch with Wolfgang and his family for all of these years, and often speak to him by phone. They have visited us and we have visited them several times.

Lydia was born July 29, 1927. She married Kurt Thurau and they have two children, *Heidrun* and *Holgar*. Kurt was a refugee from eastern Germany who came to Wiesbaden, along with his parents and a sister, just after the war. He worked in the same plant as Georg, Ria and Hans. He retired a few years ago, and has since died. Lydia has recently died also.

Ursula was born December 16, 1928, in Wiesbaden.

Georg and Frieda Maus, their three adult daughters, (Ria, Lydia and Ursula) and three grandchildren (Ingrid, Hans and Wolfgang) all lived in a four-room apartment on the ground floor of a city-owned building when I first met them. The apartment had two bedrooms, a living room, and a small kitchen. Off the hallway was a "water closet" (toilet). There was no bathroom nor was there a hot water heater. The only appliances were a coal/gas cook stove in the kitchen, and small, potbellied, coal, stoves in the living room and in each of the bedrooms. All of the rooms were furnished with very fine, handcrafted, furniture. I later learned that most German families had their homes furnished in this manner. In some households, the furniture was hundreds of years old, passed down from generation to generation. Cabinetmaking was, and still is, an exceptional craft in Germany.

All adults in the family, except Frieda, worked, but times were tough. The war had been over less than five years and the economy was still in the pits. Their diet consisted, just about entirely, of vegetables. Meat was far too expensive for working people so they had meat only about twice a month, and then only on special occasions.

But the most remarkable trait of this family was its ability to accept the American soldiers as individuals and not as the enemy. They had every reason to hate us, but they didn't. Let me explain why this is so remarkable.

As I tell this story, keep in mind that this family was a poor, working-class family. They weren't part of Hitler's "Master Race," or even of the Nazi party. In fact, Frau Maus was once jailed for three days because she had criticized Hitler in a conversation with a neighbor and another neighbor, a Nazi Captain, overheard them talking and turned her in.

The apartment building was within fifty feet of the U.S. Air Force Hospital, the largest US military hospital in Europe. In January 1981, that hospital became world-famous as the welcoming point for the U.S. Embassy hostages who had been released by Iran. It served the same purpose in later years as American hostages came back from Lebanon and other Middle East countries.

The American forces entered Wiesbaden on March 25, 1945, captured the city without resistance, and immediately took command of the military hospital. As is always the case when a conquering army enters a fallen city, total panic sets in, especially among the poor. Word had been circulated by the Nazis that the American troops would rape and plunder the city. Everyone was terrified.

Several days after the troops arrived, two American soldiers, accompanied by a German interpreter, knocked on the Maus' door. The German informed the family that the Americans were taking over the entire block of apartments for use as troop housing. The family had to be out within four hours. When asked where they should go, the German sneered, "Go up in the mountains, and cover yourselves with leaves." Then he laughed.

They left the apartment as directed. They were allowed to take only what clothes they could wear, one place setting of china and silver for each family member, and whatever food they could carry. They did manage to smuggle out their jewelry and a few prized possessions, under the babies in the baby carriages. All of their beautiful, handcrafted furniture was left behind, as well as all their dishes, their silver, and their personal possessions. Even their photo albums were left behind.

They found a place to stay with some friends for a few days, then the city leased them a two room suite in an old hotel. They lived (I should say "survived"), in temporary quarters for over two years, then the American troops vacated the apartment, and they were allowed to return.

When they returned to the apartment, everything was gone. Their lovely furniture, their good china, their stoves, everything was gone. The apartment was completely bare, except for some refuse left behind by the troops.

They started over. Little by little, they replaced the furniture and belongings and went on with their lives.

They had every reason to hate the Americans, and at first they did. But gradually, as they became acquainted with the Americans at the hospital, they began to mellow. The hatred gradually faded away.

The two youngest daughters began to date the American servicemen. They both had studied English in high school, and were reasonably fluent in the language. In 1948 **Ursula** found a clerical job at the air base. That's where I met her in December 1949.

Some Nice Places to Visit in Europe
1951-52

During the eighteen months that Ursula and I were together we traveled around the continent of Europe whenever we could. We made several trips to southern Germany, and to Holland, Belgium and Luxembourg. We also had a lot of local trips, looking at castles and monuments, and we took cruises on the Rhine River.

The trips to southern Germany were usually to Garmich-Partenkirchen, just north of the German Alps.

One March, we took a cog-train, through a tunnel in the mountain, to the top of the <u>Zugspitze,</u> the highest spot in Germany. (nearly 10,000 feet above sea level) My, what a beautiful sight. Everything was covered with snow and we could see white-capped peaks all the way to the horizon.

In September 1951, we took a 10-day bus tour to southern Germany, Austria, Switzerland, and northern Italy. It was a lovely trip through some very beautiful country. We visited Lake Constance, the Black Forest and the Rhine River Falls in Germany, Geneva and Zürich in Switzerland, Gardone, in the Italian Alps, and Venice, Italy. To get to all those beautiful places, we spent many days in the Alps.

The only drawback was that the bus, an obsolete old model from before the war, broke down several times. Each time, they put us in a hotel while they fixed the bus. All in all, we had a great time. I was the only American on the bus, except for a German-born lady from Chicago, who was traveling with her sister. Everyone was very nice, and it was a fine trip.

One evening, we stopped at a small hotel, on the side of a mountain in Switzerland. The whole busload of us walked into the hotel, where the manager was waiting to greet us. When he saw me, he smiled, opened his arms, and said, "Ah, chauffeur," thinking that I was the bus driver. Suddenly it occurred to me that I was wearing my Air Force blue uniform, as I was required to do whenever traveling in Europe. Everyone laughed, then someone told him who I was, and we had a fine evening.

****

We were at a hotel in Gardone, in the Italian Alps. It was a beautiful day, and there was a large, mountain lake, just behind the hotel. There was a nice beach and a diving board, which stuck out about 20 feet over the water. Ursula and I decided to go swimming, even though there was no one else there. There was a row of small changing rooms on the beach, so we went into one of them, and put on our bathing suits. Being the show-off that I was, I walked onto the diving board, and dove into the water. The instant that I hit the water, I knew that I had made a terrible mistake. I had failed to realize that this was a mountain lake, fed by melting snow.

I kicked myself to the surface, and swam to shore as fast as I could. Whenever Ursula told the story, she laughed and said that I ran on top of the water to get to the shore.

Maybe she was right, but even if I can walk on water, I'm not going to test my abilities again.

Colonel Whitcoph
Wiesbaden, Germany – 1951

Colonel Whitcoph, the Commander of Wiesbaden Air Base, was a legend. He had taken the base from a bombed-out pile of rubble, in 1945, to a fully rebuilt, functioning base. It was a showplace; clean, green, and immaculately groomed. He did it with strong discipline and hard work.

Most of the men despised him, but I liked him.

There was no reason for the men to hate him so. It was just that his aloof manner and ramrod personality turned the men against him. For example: One spring morning, at about 0745 hours, the Colonel looked out of his office window and observed a Second Lieutenant tossing a cigarette butt into the street. He leaped up from his chair, raced down the stairs and out of the building. He caught up with the young officer, stood him at "attention" for several minutes, and told him the facts about base cleanliness. He then directed the lieutenant to pick up every cigarette butt on over two blocks of street. The Colonel walked along with him to make sure that he did it right.

Colonel Whitcoph, being the sort of disciplinarian that he was, had done a remarkable job in making the base livable for everyone. He had built a gymnasium, a movie theater, an enlisted men's club, a bowling alley and a service club, facts that seemed to go largely unappreciated.

To manage these new facilities, he had hired a group of fine, young, energetic, American women to operate the facilities. These young women were housed in the Base Officers Quarters (BOQ), a fact that was to cause him some minor grief.

Her name was Melody Parsons, and she worked as a Hostess in the service club. It seemed that Melody had considerable experience in the field of entertainment, and she decided to put it to some use on Wiesbaden Air Base.

Colonel Whitcoph unwittingly contributed to his own problem by requiring that all new arrivals, below the rank of Major, be prohibited from leaving the base for their first three weeks after their arrival. The reasoning was that the men should have a period of indoctrination about the ways of the "natives" before they could safely venture into town. After all, everyone knew about the strong beer and the wild women in Germany. Of course he didn't realize that his age and experience level completely disqualified him to make such a judgment. Also, his wife was living with him in Germany.

Ah, yes, it's lonely at the top.

Miss Parsons opened up shop in her BOQ room. At first it was only junior officers that visited her, and then gradually, as the word spread, her business expanded. After all, since the officers were in on the action, no one complained and everything was alright. That enterprising young lady made a great deal of money before she was found out.

What brought her down was her lack of organization. Business was just too good. She should've worked by appointment, or at least posted a lookout.

It was a lovely summer night, about 2200 hrs (10 PM) and Colonel Whitcopf and his wife were taking a leisurely stroll around the base. As they approached their quarters, the Colonel noticed, what appeared to be, a line of enlisted men standing outside the door of one of the BOQ buildings. This seemed a bit odd to him, so he investigated.

Miss Melody Parsons was on her way to America the next morning.

Chapter 10

FORT SNELLING,
MINNESOTA – 1952-55

Ft. Snelling, on the edge of St. Paul, Minnesota, was originally built by settlers in the days of the Indian Wars and at some point a military installation had been built south of the original fort. It's the same Ft. Snelling that I mentioned earlier in this book when I described my enlistment in the Army Air Corps in 1946.

When I got there this time the buildings of the old Army base were being used by the 31st Air Division, and it was called Ft. Snelling Air Force Base. In addition to the original buildings, a large brick, windowless, building had been built, to serve as the Command Center for the North Central Area of the Air Defense Command. The 31st Air Division had airbases, with jet-fighter aircraft, at Sioux City, Iowa, Duluth, Minnesota, and Sioux Falls, South Dakota, plus a fighter squadron at the Minneapolis-St. Paul International Airport. Also under the jurisdiction of the 31st Air Division were numerous radar stations, used for tracking of all aircraft flying across North Central United States, and southern Canada. Those were the years of the "Cold War" and our military forces were on constant alert.

When I got to Ft. Snelling, I checked in at the personnel office and was told that I was being assigned to the office of the 31st Air Division Inspector General, and that my supervisor would be Captain Radke, the Division Provost Marshal, and the top cop in the Air Division.

I talked with my new boss for a while then went house hunting.

Finding a place to live was a new experience for me and I had a tough time getting the job done. I had never been responsible for a family home, so I was at a loss as to what to do.

I had left Ursula with my parents in Fairmont, Minnesota, so I was in a bit of a hurry to find a place. To begin with, I had lived in military barracks ever since I entered the service and I had never lived in a city in my life. I didn't have the foggiest notion of how to look for something to live in, and especially a place good enough for my new bride.

I looked at newspaper ads, talked to people, and went to look at houses and apartments. On the second day, I rented an upstairs, furnished, apartment in a private home, then drove to Fairmont, picked up Ursula and drove back to St. Paul. All of our personal belongings had been shipped to Ft. Snelling, so we made arrangements to have them delivered to the apartment, and we moved in.

I had been away from Minnesota quite a while, so I didn't realize just how cold it could get in January. The first morning that I got up, to go to work, it was 14° below zero. Our Hudson was parked at the curb, in a snow bank, and it simply wouldn't start. I called my boss and told him that I would be late for work, then called a towing service. The tow-truck driver connected his jumper cables to the battery, and started the car. Then he pulled the car out of the snow bank and I went to work. I was thinking, "Welcome back to Minnesota."

My new job was a mixture of about everything that had to do with military security. I processed security clearance paperwork for a lot of people, kept track of the people who were in the stockades at our three airbases and did inspections of the Air Police operations in conjunction with the overall function of the Inspector General.

Because of the nature of my work, the first thing that I did was to fill out paperwork for a Top Secret security clearance. Basically, that means that I had access to any and all documents, conversations, or equipment, with that classification, or lower, provided that I had official authorization to work with the information.

One of the most interesting things that I did at Fort Snelling was to help with security checks within the headquarters area. Both Captain Radke and I carried identification papers signed by the Commanding General of the 31st Air Division. Those papers specifically identified what we could investigate, and how to handle what we found.

Every now and then, we casually walked through offices to determine if security procedures were in place to properly safeguard the classified documentation within the facility.

One day we walked into an open-bay office, and found that everyone in the office had gone to lunch. I walked over to the corner of the room, to a cubicle where the Officer-in-Charge worked, glanced around the cubicle and noticed that one drawer of his safe was slightly open. I reached in, took out a classified document, and then walked out of the cubicle and out of the building. When we got back to our office we showed the document to the Inspector General and told him where we had gotten it. He directed Captain Radke to take the document to the Commanding General, and to tell him where it had been recovered. The officer from whom I had taken the document was severely reprimanded, even though he swore that he had not left his safe open when he went to lunch.

A couple of times, on rainy days, we put on raincoats, to hide our identity, and placed simulated bombs in strategic places, such as alongside the wheels of fighter aircraft. Each bomb was made up of a brick, wrapped in ordinary wrapping paper, on which we had written our names, our phone number, and the word, "BOMB." When we got to a site that we had selected, we casually walked to where we wanted to place the bomb, wrote the exact date and time on the brick, placed it in plain sight, and walked away. After we got back to our office, we called the people responsible for the security of the area and told them where we had placed the "BOMB." Of course, they immediately sent someone one out to find the bomb. Usually, they called us, and apologized for their lack of security. In most cases, no further action was taken, however if the person who called was belligerent, the General was told about it.

It wasn't necessary to do those stunts very often because the word soon got out, and security was immediately brought up to standard.

Now for my home life while we were in St. Paul.

Once we got moved in and took a better look at the place that I had rented, we knew that I had really goofed up. It was the first place that I had ever rented and it was obvious that I wasn't experienced in such matters. Thinking back on it, I wonder why Ursula didn't just leave me and go back to Germany. What I had rented was much worse than the crowded apartment that she had grown up in.

But Ursula was a real trooper. She just buckled down and cleaned up the place.

The woman who owned the house, and who lived downstairs, was a real nut-case. Every day, she gave Ursula a hard time about something. It took us only a couple weeks to realize that we had to move. I came up with a story that I was getting transferred, and being as dumb as she was, she agreed to cancel our lease. By that time we had already located an apartment in a three-story building near downtown St. Paul.

We moved there and were very comfortable. Ursula found a job as a clerk in an insurance office, close enough so that she could walk to work, and we were as cozy as any newlyweds could be.

We had been there less than a year, when a two-story building directly behind our apartment building caught fire, and the fire got hot enough to break the windows in our apartment and char the window sills. The major damage to our place was not from the fire, but from the firemen trying to put out the fire. Our bed was smashed to the floor, and the whole apartment needed repair work and paint. We moved to a hotel for about two weeks while the place was being fixed up.

Now let's look at some pure, simple, stupidity. We had a perfectly good 1949 Hudson automobile that we had bought in Washington but I decided that we just had to have a new car. I had never owned a new car and in my mind, it was a necessity. So, with the help of a finance company, we bought a new, 1953 Ford Crown Victoria hardtop convertible. For the first time in my life, I had a new car, but I was also deeply in debt.

When I woke up and realized that my income was far short of meeting our expenses, I started looking for a part-time job to supplement our income. While I was in Germany, I had gotten interested in the sport of bowling, so I went to a bowling alley in St. Paul and asked them if they needed any help in the evenings. The lady who ran the place had been looking for help and I was hired as a pinsetter, seven nights a week, from 8 to 11 o'clock. You younger folks probably don't know that, in those ancient days, there were no automatic pin setting machines in bowling alleys, and all of the pins were picked up and put in the racks by boys and men who were very nimble.

I had set pins for only about a week, when I was promoted to assistant manager of the bowling alley. That meant that I came in about 7:30 at night and worked the front desk until about 11:00. I held that job for the rest of the time we were in St. Paul.

I could tell a lot of stories about what happened while I worked at that bowling alley, but you probably wouldn't believe them, so I won't waste your time.

After two years, we determined that, even with my part-time job, we couldn't live on the pay I was making in the United States, so we decided to go back overseas.

In January 1955, I applied for an overseas assignment, with a preference for Europe. To my surprise and pleasure, I was assigned to the 7493rd Special Investigations Wing, Rhein-Main, Germany, with duty station at OSI District 5 in Paris, France. I didn't know much about the Office of Special Investigations (OSI), except that it was what you might call "the FBI of the Air Force." I assumed that one of the reasons I was selected for that assignment was that I had a Top-Secret security clearance, a requirement to be assigned to OSI.

As soon as I got my shipping orders, Ursula put in for her US citizenship. The normal waiting period for citizenship was several years, but because I was military and I had received orders for overseas duty, the waiting period was waived, and she received her US citizenship before we left St. Paul.

When she went back to Europe, with her US passport, she was a very proud American lady.

Following are some stories about Ft Snelling and about someone that we met on the way to Paris.

Hoss Mullins
Ft. Snelling, Minnesota

This story has two central characters, Sergeant Hoss Mullens and Airman Second Class Jane Benson. They were in the same Air Force unit, but didn't know each other very well. They were thrown together by an event that changed their lives.

Hoss Mullens' given name was Jerome, but scarcely anybody knew what it was. He simply looked so much like a horse that no one bothered to ask him what his real name was. He had a long, narrow, face and a huge nose that sort of drooped toward his upper lip. His resemblance to a prairie bronco was remarkable. He even had the sad eyes of a bronco. And to add to the impersonation, he was only five feet, four inches tall and weighed nearly 180 pounds, all muscle. He was twenty-eight years old, but most of his hair had begun to depart, leaving only a fringe around the edges and a tassel in the center, just above his eyes.

Hoss was a peach of a guy. He was quiet and friendly, and except when he got drunk, he was a joy to be around. Everybody liked him.

But, because of his ugly appearance, Hoss was just not attractive to women. No one could remember ever seeing him with a girl, or for that matter, even seeing him leave the base. His life centered on his work, the weight room in the gym and the Non-Commissioned Officers club. During the week, he worked hard all day, built muscles in the gym a couple hours each night, then went to his room in the barracks and read himself to sleep. But weekends were different. Every Saturday night, he went to the NCO Club right after supper, played cards, and drank beer until he got too drunk to play anymore. Sometime toward midnight he staggered back to the barracks and went to bed, where he usually remained until reveille on Monday morning.

Jane Benson was a rather large girl, born and raised on a South Dakota farm. She was what you might call "plain." Her hair was brown and worn page-boy; and her complexion was pitted by too many years of sweets and cokes. Her uniform was usually wrinkled and didn't fit her plump frame very well. She was twenty-two years old and had been in the Air Force for nearly three years. Jane was a nice kid but because of her appearance, she had very few dates.

To understand this story you need to know a little about the physical layout of the base.

The airmen's living area consisted of eight barracks, standing in a row, perpendicular to the street and twenty-five feet apart. Each barracks was a wood-framed, white, slate-sided building, two stories high. Each housed about fifty people in one and two person rooms. As you approached the living area from the business section of the air base, you came first to three women's barracks, then to five men's barracks. In front of the line of buildings were a sidewalk and a parking area.

It was a warm, balmy, Saturday night in July. Jane had been in town during the day and had returned to her room just after supper. She loafed around the barracks, doing laundry, ironing, and cleaning until about 11:00. As she prepared for bed, she pulled the shade down, removed her clothing, put on her robe, and went down the hall to take a shower.

At about the time that Jane was doing her laundry, Hoss was at the club, getting cleaned in a poker game. He also was becoming very drunk. He was the type of person who tended to drink in inverse proportion to his card playing success, and that night he was getting skunked. By 11:00 he was too drunk to continued, so he quit the game and headed toward the barracks.

As he staggered down the street it became apparent to him that his bladder was full. He looked around to see if anybody was looking, then sauntered over to the side of the nearest barracks, opened his fly, and proceeded to urinate against the wall of the building. He didn't realize that his eyes were at exactly the correct level to look under the shade into Jane's room. He was probably the only man on the base that was short enough to see under the shade without stooping over. But he didn't know any of this. He was so drunk that he didn't even know where he was, or know what he was seeing. He continued with his chore.

Jane returned from the shower, entered the room, and closed the door. She slipped out of her robe and reached into the closet for her pajamas. From out of the corner of her eye, she saw two bloodshot eyes peering at her from under the window shade.

For the next few seconds there was chaos.

Jane clasped her robe against her nakedness. She screamed and pointed toward the window. She was too terrified to do anything else. She continued screaming. Doors flew open and every woman in the barracks added her voice to the chorus.

Hoss' earlier bad luck was still with him. Just as Jane screamed, an Air Police patrol car drove past the barracks. Poor Hoss was still standing there, organ in hand, when the Air Policeman nabbed him. He tried to get someone to tell him what was happening; he had not even heard the screams. Only when he sobered up the next morning, in the stockade, did he comprehend the seriousness of his crime.

Hoss was court-martialed for conduct unbecoming a Non-Commissioned Officer, reduced in grade to Basic Airman and restricted to the base for thirty days. The base restriction meant nothing to him since he never left the base anyway. He served his sentence without complaint.

After the excitement died down, Jane began to consider what had happened. She began to feel sorry for poor Hoss. After all, he hadn't hurt her; hadn't even intended to do her any harm. Whenever she thought of being gazed at, in all her nakedness, she even felt a bit tingly. Soon she began to feel guilty. She had ruined the career of a nice guy who never hurt anybody. She felt terrible and decided to try to make it up to him.

At first it was only an occasional nod or greeting in passing. Then Jane began visiting him in his office at Base Supply and soon they were having coffee together every day. After about two months, Hoss got up enough nerve to ask Mary for a date, the first date he had ever had. She accepted.

Less than a year later, they were married. When their enlistments were up, they left the Air Force and moved to Oklahoma. I never saw them again, but I heard that they had settled on a ranch and were busy raising two little ponies.

Sergeant Cyrus Lyshek
North Atlantic – 1955

This story concerns someone that I met while crossing the North Atlantic on a troopship.

On June 14, 1955, in New York, Ursula and I bordered a troopship, bound for Bremerhaven, Germany.

One of the nicest things that happened on that ship was that we met Sergeant First Class Cy Lyshek, his wife Maureen and their three children. We became instant friends with them and we communicated with them for many years.

Cy Lyshek was one of the sharpest soldiers that I've ever met. He had been a combat infantryman during World War II and in Korea he had worked in graves registration, the unit that picks up the dead soldier's bodies and sends them home. It's the worst job in the Army. He said that he would rather be shot than have to pick up those wrecked bodies.

Maureen told us that he very seldom slept well, and frequently woke up screaming and sweating.

Cy put in a three-year tour in Europe after we met, then moved through several assignments, including two tours in Vietnam. In Vietnam, he served as a forward artillery observer, the guy who hides between enemy lines, and directs the artillery strikes.

In all of the combat of three wars he was never wounded, but his mind took a terrible beating.

Many years later, he retired from the Army, with over 30 years of service.

About nine months after he retired, he died, peacefully, in his sleep.

Chapter 11

PARIS, FRANCE – 1955-58

We arrived in Paris in June of 1955.

After a visit to my office, Ursula took the train to Wiesbaden, so she could live with her family until I could find a place for us to live. Then I went to work at OSI District 5.

During the time that Ursula was in Wiesbaden, I spent my leisure time wandering around the city. I worked all week but each weekend I did such things as; strolling about the Champs-Elysees or going up to the various levels of the Eiffel Tower and looked out over the city. I walked around quite a bit and found that Paris was a beautiful city, with the River Seine wondering through it. All through the center of the city, the banks of the river are formed by concrete walls, bordered by about a 20-foot wide strip of brick paving. Along that strip are many shops and food stands, so that tourists can relax as they stroll along the river. It's a very peaceful and quiet place to spend some time.

I found a small apartment in the section of Paris called Montmartre, which is high on a hill overlooking the city. The area, in addition to being a residential area, was historical and had a well-known artist colony. Just outside of our apartment, on any given day, you could find artists painting a scene of something interesting. This was the area where the famous artist, Vincent van Gogh lived and worked most of his life.

The apartment that I rented had a living room, with a built-in bed in a niche on one side, a kitchen, large enough to eat in, and a bathroom. Even though it was small, it was quite comfortable and unique. As soon as we received our things from St. Paul, Ursula came back from Germany and we were nice and snug in our new home.

There were no English-speaking television stations within range of Paris, and if there had been, I suppose we wouldn't have bothered to hookup to one. We read a lot, we talked a lot, and we listened to Radio-Free-Europe. We spent many days wandering about the city, and since I had been there for over a month and had done some sightseeing, I knew pretty much where to go to find interesting tourist attractions.

Unfortunately for us, the winter of 1955–56, was one of the coldest in many years, and the little gas heater in our apartment couldn't keep up with the cold. For days at a time, it was very cold and Ursula had her legs frozen again, like she did when she was a young woman, We knew that we couldn't stay there another winter, and started looking for a better apartment.

One of our OSI Interpreters learned that we were looking for a new place to live, and he told me about an apartment in the suburban town of Sevre. The apartment was owned by an American man and his French wife, and they were returning to the United States, so that he could teach at a university in Louisiana. It was a very nice place with a bedroom, living room, kitchen and bath, located on the second floor of a two-story apartment building overlooking a large forest. From a small balcony off of the kitchen, we could look out over the town, and from our bedroom window, we could look into the forest. We lived in that apartment until we went back to the US in October, 1958.

Now, back to what I did at OSI District 5.

The Air Force Office of Special Investigations was organized in 1948 as the Air Force investigative agency under the direct control of the Inspector General, US Air Force. Every Air Force base in the world had at least one OSI Special Agent located there.

My work at OSI was the most interesting work that I have ever done. Our District Office was in Paris, and we had Detachments at all of the 9 airbases in France. I was the NCOIC of the Administrative Division and supervised 10 of the greatest guys that ever served in the Air Force. We, like most OSI people, wore civilian clothes, usually business suits, to work every day. They all worked as many hours as they were asked to work, and I never heard one of them complain about anything. They ranged in rank from Airman Second Class to Master Sergeant. Most of them were clerks, but we also had a photographer, an interpreter, and a Supply Sergeant. In addition to their regular jobs, they performed duties in just about anything that you can imagine. Some of those clerks later became OSI Special Agents.

My duties were quite widespread. In addition to being the office manager, I maintained the security of the office, including a couple dozen four-drawer, fireproof, safes. Those safes were all filled with classified documents pertaining to OSI investigative activities. I took it upon myself to learn how those combination locks worked, and soon learned how to reset the locks, and how to get into them, if the combinations were forgotten or lost.

As I mentioned earlier, I had a high security clearance, and nearly everything we touched was classified. There is one big problem with that situation. People who deal with classified information in the military aren't allowed to discuss their work with anyone who doesn't have the proper security clearance, so for the next 12 years, until I retired from the Air Force, Ursula never knew exactly what I did during my workday. For the same reason, I will not be able to tell you much about what I did during those 12 years. I've been out of the Air Force since 1967, but I still won't discuss any classified information, even if I could remember it. I can, however tell about some of the nitty-gritty, and some of the fun things that happened while I was with OSI.

My first year in Paris, I worked about 60 hours a week. When I got there, the man that I replaced had been gone for over three months. The work had piled up, and the discipline and morale were in terrible shape. As I walked into the office on my first day of duty, the first thing that I saw was two Staff Sergeants, standing face-to-face, yelling at each other. To add to that problem, within the year, due to normal rotations, back to the States, my workforce of 10 men had dropped to only six. Some of the men worked as much overtime as I did. As you can well imagine, they were terribly overworked. The personnel problem was caused by the fact that our Commanding Officer, for reasons unknown to me, transferred any new man, who was not Caucasian, to one of our detachments, instead of to my office, where he belonged.

The manpower problem was solved about a year after I got there, when Lt. Col. L.L. Free, was transferred in as our new Commanding Officer. He understood the situation immediatly and started moving those troops from the detachments into my office. Soon our strength was back to normal. Col. Free was an excellent commander and leader. As his top noncommissioned officer, I was responsible to him for the actions of the men under my supervision, and his door was always open to me.

Just a note about Col. Free. Four years later, after Col. Free had moved to the OSI Directorate, in Washington, and I was at OSI District 4, in Maryland, he arranged to have me transferred to work for him in the Plans and Policy Division of the Directorate. Seven years after that, when I retired from the Air Force, and he was Deputy Director for Operations, he personally arranged to conduct my retirement ceremony. During the ceremony, he spent several minutes telling the audience about how I had "broken him in" to his job in Paris. It was a great honor to work for Col. Free. He was the finest officer that I knew during my 20 years in the Air Force.

Paris was a great place to visit but not such a great place to live, because we had no money to spend on the good times that were available. We did manage to see the Folies Bergere, and we toured most of the free places, but otherwise we just went to a lot of English-speaking movies. We went to Germany a couple times a year to visit Ursula's family and we went to Belgium and Holland once, but otherwise we were just like poor tourists.

In November 1956, I was sent to a six-week course at the Noncommissioned Officers Academy, in Freising, Germany. The Academy was sort of an officer's training school for senior sergeants. It was somewhat like the military academies, with hazing, strict discipline, rigid inspections, etc. I had always liked close-order drill and the last week of training I was chosen, by the men of my 50-man flight, to lead our flight at a drill competition. It was a timed competition, so I memorized a routine that would execute as many different commands as possible, without wasting time walking. We practiced for hours and hours and we thought that we were really good. During the competition, I gave 43 different commands, all properly executed, in three minutes, but we didn't win. We were disappointed, but we were still very proud of the way we performed. Those of you, who have been in the military, try to remember 43 commands from the Drill Manual.

I graduated from the Academy on December 16, returned to Paris, and then immediately took emergency leave to see my mother, who was dying of cancer. I stayed with my parents in Fairmont for two weeks, said my final goodbye to Mom, and then flew back to Paris to complete the rest of my tour. Mom died August 21, 1958.

Just before I went to the NCO Academy, Ursula discovered that she was pregnant. We had always wanted a family, but the doctors in St. Paul had told her she could not have children because of a glandular problem. She had been through many tests and had some very expensive treatments, but nothing worked. Anyway, she finally got pregnant and you have never seen a happier woman. Unfortunately, she had a miscarriage while I was on leave in Minnesota. She soon got pregnant again, and miscarried again. After the second miscarriage, I went to Col. Free and told him that I thought that my wife wasn't getting good care at the American Hospital. Col. Free called the Commanding Officer of the hospital and arranged for me to go to see him. The hospital commander discussed her case with me and told me that he agreed that she was probably not getting the best of care. He told me that he had a new doctor, who had studied glandular problems, and that he would assign him to Ursula's case. She soon became pregnant again, and Carol Jean was born August 8, 1958.

When I went to the French authorities to register Carol's birth, I had a hard time convincing them that Carol Jean was a girl. J-e-a-n is the spelling of the male French name pronounced "John."

I received my orders for assignment to OSI District 4, Suitland, Maryland, just a few miles south of Washington, DC, so on October 13, 1958, Ursula, Carol and I boarded a Navy C-54, at Orly Field, in Paris and flew to McGuire Air Force Base, New Jersey.

Following are some stories about Paris.

Culture Shock
Paris, France – 1955

A great way to spend a hot afternoon in Paris is to visit the Eiffel Tower. It's always cool on the upper levels and the people-watching is great.

The ground level of the tower complex, where the legs touch the ground, is in the center of a large park covering several acres. Around the legs are several small shops, the rest rooms, and other service facilities.

The first level, about fifty feet from the ground, is mostly just a restaurant. It's a favorite dining spot of the French and of the tourists who have lots of money.

The second level, about 100 feet from the ground, is the best place from which to see the city. The entire area is open, with only a steel railing around the outer edge. There is plenty of room to walk around. On all four sides are coin-operated telescopes to assist in your viewing of the city. Also at this level are a few small souvenir shops and lunch stands.

The third, or top, level is a small, glass-enclosed, compartment, over 300 feet from the ground. Although it's a thrill to go to the top, you can't see much from there. It's too crowded and the glass obstructs the view. I went up there only once.

All levels can be reached by elevator. If you are very young, or very foolish, you can walk up a stairway as far as the second level. I walked up only one time. I was only twenty-seven years old and thought that I was pretty macho to tackle this monumental task. By the time I reached the second level, I had learned the meaning of the word "stupid."

On my first weekend in Paris, I decided to visit the tower. I was alone in the city, so I was free to do anything I wanted to do. It was at the tower that I received the first of several cultural shocks that I was to receive while in Paris.

I was lounging about the park at the base of the tower when the call of nature visited me. I began to panic. I had no idea where a restroom was, or what name would be on the men's room door. Anyone who has traveled in a foreign country will recognize the dilemma. In search of relief, I dashed over to a cluster of buildings near one leg of the tower. I spotted a small building that looked like it might be a restroom, so I immediately headed in that direction. The building had two doors but neither had a name. I anxiously stood and waited. Several women went into the door on the left, so I assumed the one on the right was for men. I went in, and sure enough, I was in a public restroom, just like any other, except for one difference. Sitting by the door was a shabbily clad old woman, a roll of toilet paper in her hand. Her presence jolted me a bit, but I was in too much of a hurry to care. I headed for one of the booths, but the old woman stopped me. "Papier, monsieur?", she said, holding out two sheets of toilet paper with one hand and extending her other hand, obviously asking for money. I suppose that she was familiar with tourists. I handed her a French coin (probably too much), grabbed the paper, and dashed into a booth.

I had barely gotten seated when I heard a clatter of high heels approaching. "Was I in the ladies room?" I thought. The heels came closer. "Do they arrest Peeping Toms in France?" I thought. The door to the booth next to mine opened and closed. A heeled shoe, with a very shapely ankle above it, was placed just six inches from my foot. I heard water running. "Oh my God, how am I going to get out of this? I'm in the wrong damn toilet and I can't even speak the language." I'm not a very stable person, especially when faced with situations that are beyond my understanding. My concerns about nature vanished. I jerked up my trousers and fled. I was half way back to the hotel before I notice that my fly was still open.

Of course, what I had failed to comprehend was that in France, many public restrooms are unisex.

A New Acquaintance
Paris, France – 1955

For the first few days in Paris, I nearly starved. I spoke no French, and for some reason, most of the waiters refused to speak English.

About the fourth day on the job, I heard about the Capri Bar. I was told that they had good food and that it was a friendly place. How friendly, I was to find out later.

That night after work I went there to see if I could satisfy my craving for a steak.

The Capri Bar was located about fifty feet off the Champs Elysees on Rue Washington. The front section was a small stand-up bar with room for about ten people. In one corner there stood a pinball machine. Behind the barroom was a larger room, perhaps twenty by thirty feet, which served as a restaurant and party room.

The bar had a regular clientele of mostly American GIs and English speaking students. It also served as a home base for two $100-a-day call girls and a few street girls. The street girls used the bar as a resting place between tricks, and the call girls used the bar's phone as a business phone.

The Capri Bar had been a home-away-from-home for our unit for many years. On any given night, some of the men from our outfit could be found eating dinner and/or drinking there. The married men often brought their wives. The single men used the bar as a home port during their evenings on the town, but very seldom used the services of the girls that hung out there. The two call girls were priced out of their range anyway and they all were just sort of pals to all of us.

I suppose that I should stop here and explain a little about the French lifestyle, so you won't think that we were all sex-starved alcoholics on a perpetual orgy.

Prostitution in Paris was (and still is, I suppose) a way of life. Those girls at the bar were just young, friendly kids who happened to make their living on the streets. They were neatly dressed and well mannered. They respected our wives and never even hinted at propositioning the married men. We were very comfortable as a group. Ursula and I visited that bar, off and on, for over three years and enjoyed ourselves every time.

Now, back to my story.

I walked in and sat down in the back room. I was about three hours early for the normal French dinner hour, so I was the only person in the room. The bartender, acting as waiter, came over and I ordered a beer and a steak dinner. He brought the beer and I settled back to relax.

I had just gotten settled when this sweet young thing, about 18 years old, walked in. She looked around the room, spotted me, and came over. She spun around, flipped up her skirt in back, and sat down across the table from me. I couldn't help but notice her black, lace panties.

"IIi, I'm Mary Ann," she purred, "You alone?"

I don't know what I replied. I think I nodded my head.

Mary Ann took care of my shyness. She came right out with what was on her mind.

"You go with me, huh?" she said. Her English wasn't very good.

"No, thank you," I replied.

"Oh, come on, you go with me," she persisted.

"No" I said, getting a bit peeved.

"Please you go with me?" she pleaded. "I just got done with my period and had a douche. You be the first one."

Now, I've been around the block a few times, but this gal was something else. I started to sweat. I tried to think of something to say.

I finally said, "I've never paid for it yet and I'm not going to start now." I could feel my face getting red.

She cocked her head to one side, a mischievous grin beginning to develop.

"You married?" she asked.

I nodded.

"You pay - - you pay," she said. Then she laughed, stood up, flipped her skirt again, and swept out of the room and onto the street.

My steak dinner came a few minutes later and I managed to get it down. I was a bit shaken, but soon I began to relax and enjoy my meal.

The Crusade of Brad Anderson
Paris, France – 1956-58

Doctors tell us that we need at least eight hours of sleep each day to maintain our health and to carry on normal activities. Airman 1st Class Brad Anderson got about sixteen hours of sleep a <u>week,</u> during his three years in Paris. He usually slept during the day on Saturdays and Sundays but the rest of the time he slept very little.

When Brad came to Paris he was eighteen years old and looked even younger. When he left he was twenty-one, and looked forty. I suspect that the lack of sleep had something to do with it.

Brad was a rather smallish man; about five-feet-five, 140 pounds, and quite handsome, in a boyish sort of way. French women found him attractive, a fact that nearly destroyed him.

Apparently, when Brad first arrived in Paris he made a promise, to himself, that he would create happiness in the heart, and satisfaction in the body, of every unmarried woman in the city. I think that he nearly succeeded.

And so he started on his crusade.

Paris was a city that never slowed down. Normal working hours were from nine until noon, and from three until seven or eight at night.

The three hour noon-break served as a time for eating, for napping, and for cuddling with your mistress. Each night the restaurants served dinner from eight to midnight. The bars never closed.

Unfortunately for Brad, we Americans worked from 8:00 to 5:00. That made it very difficult for a man, of his persuasion, to accomplish what he set out to do and still get some sleep. The only leisure time he had was between 5:00 P.M. and 10:00 P.M., when the dinner rush slowed down. During that time he took care of personal business such as laundry and groceries. Since he was merely a GI in a foreign land, he had very little money to spend on luxuries. He had to save his money for his crusade.

His typical schedule started the evening with bar hopping until he found the woman that he was going to service, then an hour or so of drinks and conversation, hopefully ending in a bed somewhere. His batting average was better than that of Ted Williams. With a little luck, they would be in bed by one or two in the morning. If his first attempt failed, he would simply start over. You'd think that this schedule would allow for a couple hours of sleep each night, but Brad was very thorough in his work. Also, he seemed to invariably pick up women with considerable stamina.

Along about 5:00 A.M. he wandered back to his apartment, took a shower, and got ready to go to work. Each morning he proclaimed to each of us, that he was through with that sort of life and he was going to sleep for at least eight hours the next night. He never did. When quitting time arrived, he was primed and ready to go again.

I could never understand how he did it. He was a good worker who always completed his assignments correctly and on time, and he was always cheerful and courteous. He was a mystery.

One Friday night Brad was on Rue Pigale searching for someone who could use his services. He had been cruising the bars for about three hours when he spotted a small, basement bar that seemed to have a lot of female traffic. He smiled to himself, thinking that he had hit onto something pretty amazing. There were very few men around, and he had the field to himself.

Brad went into the bar and sat down at a table. He surveyed the place with a professional eye and liked what he saw. Everywhere he looked there were beautiful women. He was truly a stranger in paradise.

He picked out an especially attractive blond, who was seated at the bar, went over, and perched on the stool next to her. He struck up a conversation. She seemed friendly, but a bit aloof. After five minutes or so, he decided to make his move. He placed his arm around her shoulders and said, "You look lonely, wanna go someplace else."

She smiled but did not speak.

That was the last thing Brad knew until he realized that he was laying on the floor, on his back. His head was spinning; he was groggy and confused.

Standing over him was a very large brunette, the tallest and meanest looking woman Brad had ever seen. She was wearing black leather jeans and jacket and around her waist was a wide motorcycle belt. She glared down at him and snarled, "Leave her alone, buster, she's mine." She turned her back on Brad and lumbered over to the bar, picked up the little blond in her arms and walked out the back door.

Poor Brad. In his amorous pursuits, he had stumbled into a lesbian bar.

As far as I know, that was the only night in three years that Brad went to bed alone.

One Hundred Dollars of Happiness
Paris, France – 1957

John was a great lover; at least, that's what <u>he</u> thought. He had been in Paris a couple of years when I got there and he knew his way around quite well. His success ratio was pretty good but there was one woman he had been trying to conquer for over two years, without success.

That woman was Kitty, one of the $100 a day call girls that operated out of the Capri Bar. He could've paid for her services, but it was against his code, as a lover, to have to pay for his pleasure. Besides that, he was only a sergeant and he really couldn't afford it.

To add to his dilemma, he was getting ready to go home for discharge and it really hurt him to leave a woman of her caliber behind without showing her what it meant to have a REAL man. He told us of his problem. We couldn't help him.

As we usually did when one of the boys was rotating back to the states, we planned a party for him at the Capri Bar. All of the troops and most of the wives were there. The booze flowed freely. Everyone was happy except John. He still hadn't made it with Kitty and he only had one more night to go. His flight left the next morning.

Then the idea hit us. We decided to take up a collection and buy Kitty's services for the night. Of course we wouldn't tell John of our scheme. He could go home thinking that his charm and great physical ability had conquered one of the finest and most beautiful women in Paris.

And so it was done. Very quietly, we passed the hat and collected $100. One of the guys found Kitty and told her of the plot.

Kitty went along with the scheme, for after all, she was a pro, and John was a pretty decent guy.

Kitty came into the room, went over to John, and sat on his lap, her arm around his neck. She twirled her finger around his ear and whispered, "I'm going to miss you, baby; let's go to my place. I've always wanted to find out if you're as good as the girls say you are."

She got up from his lap, took his hand, and led him out the door.

John went home a happy man.

Chapter 12

WASHINGTON, DC – 1958-1967

We landed at McGuire AFB, New Jersey, told a taxi driver to take us to a Plymouth dealer, and we bought a new, 1958 Plymouth sedan. We stayed overnight at McGuire and then headed west to Minnesota, to visit my Dad.

Three days later we were in Fairmont, Minnesota, visiting my father for three weeks. While we were in Paris, we had decided that we probably would have the best chance of having good living conditions, in the Washington area, if we bought a mobile home. So while we were in Fairmont, we visited a dealer and bought a 2-bedroom trailer, completely furnished, and arranged to have it delivered, direct from the factory, to Suitland, Maryland.

We lived in a trailer park near Upper Marlboro, Maryland, for a little over a year, and then moved to the base trailer park on Bolling Air Force Base, in Washington. We had a nice, corner, lot and paid only $21 a month, including electricity, water, and sewer services. We lived in the Base Trailer Park until I retired from the Air Force in 1967.

Trailer living is a good way to live when money is tight. One of the important things in life is to live the best that you can with whatever money you have.

During my time at OSI District Office 4, I was the assistant to the Training Officer, helping with the training of OSI Special Agents.

On the day before Thanksgiving 1960, the Commanding Officer of DO 4 received a phone call from Col. L. L. Free, my former boss in Paris, who had recently become the Chief, Plans and Policy Division, Air Force Office of Special Investigations, in Washington. The gist of the conversions was that Col. Free wanted me working in his office the next Monday morning.

So I went to work in the OSI Directorate, located in Temporary Building E, at 4th Street & Adams Drive, about four blocks from the US Capitol building.

Col Free's Chief Clerk had lost accountability for some classified documents, and had been removed from duty. Within a few weeks, I located all of the documents, and established accountability for them. What had happened was that the documents really weren't missing, but the record-keeping was so sloppy that nobody knew exactly where they were.

The title was, "Chief Clerk," and the task was to be the administrator of the Division, including maintaining security for all classified material in the Division.

After about three years on the job I decided that the workload wasn't heavy enough to keep me busy, so I started looking for a new position within the Division. I had been observing what the six, officer-grade, Special Agents were doing as they wrote and/or updated the OSI operating manuals, and I felt that I could fit in there someplace. The set of manuals consisted of one book for each type of investigation, plus an administrative manual. I was moved to a different Section, within the Division, and became the writer of the Administrative Manual, the document that covered all administrative procedures used in OSI investigative operations.

At, this point, I'd like to pause and mention that, all during the time that I was at the OSI Directorate, I was frequently called upon for small special assignments outside of my normal duties. They were always very interesting.

There is a tremendous amount of paperwork necessary to operate a worldwide police force; therefore, the administrative manual was quite large. It had originally been written before my time, but it was continually being updating.

In early 1965, the 1st Sgt of the 1005th Special Investigations Group, the holding organization for all people who worked in the OSI Directorate, was transferred to Alaska. With the approval of my

Division Chief, I went to the Executive Officer and told him that I would like to have the job of 1ˢᵗ Sgt, with the understanding that I would do that job in addition to being the writer of the administrative manual. The next day I assumed the additional duties of the 1ˢᵗ Sgt. I filled both positions until I retired.

One day I was talking to the Director's Executive Officer, when he suddenly looked me in the eye, smiled and said, "How you doin', Smokey?" I was quite startled; I hadn't used that alias since back 1948, in North Dakota. We laughed for a bit and I told him about how I had picked up the alias. That incident showed me just how thorough OSI investigates the background of each of their people. I had always known that OSI was a good organization, but that incident reinforced my pride in being where I was.

Now for a look at my home life in Washington.

In the summer of 1959, we had realized that living expenses were pretty tight, so I started working part-time in the Washington suburbs, mowing lawns nearly every weekend during the summer and shoveling snow in the winter. I continued with this part-time work for the rest of the time that I was in Washington.

Soon after we moved onto Bolling AFB, I decided to get some additional formal education, so I enrolled at the Capitol Institute of Technology (CIT), a small, privately owned school, located in the northwestern part of Washington. They tested my mathematics and physics skills, and I tested well enough to be accepted.

I went to school three hours a night, three nights a week, for over seven years, graduating with an Associate Degree (three year) in Electronic Engineering Technology, on December 17, 1967, just 16 days after I retired from the Air Force. My grades were good, but not quite good enough to graduate with honors. With working full time in the Air Force, going to school three nights a week, and doing yard work every weekend, my grades dropped from A's in the first year to mid B's when I graduated.

Many years ago CIT moved to a new campus in Landover, Maryland and is now named Capitol Technical University. It's now nationally recognized as a leader in the field of cyber security.

Early in my last quarter of college, a recruiter from the Western Electric Company, a wholly owned subsidiary of AT&T, visited my school, looking for students to be hired as technical writers. He looked over the upcoming graduation list and had the school officials call me in for an interview. That was on a Thursday, and the next Monday, I was in Winston-Salem, North Carolina. They offered me a starting salary that was more than double that which I was receiving from the Air Force, and I accepted the job.

In mid-November, 1967, we drove to Winston-Salem, rented a house, bought the furniture to fill it, and went back to Washington. In the last week of November, we had our personal belongings packed and shipped, sold the trailer, and moved into temporary quarters in the Navy housing project, just outside of Bolling Air Force Base.

I retired from the Air Force on December 1, 1967.

The next day we drove to Winston-Salem. The real estate agent, who had helped us find the house that we had rented, had arranged to have our furniture moved in, and when we got there we walked into a totally furnished house. All we needed to add were the kitchen utensils and some small pieces of furniture that had been shipped from Washington. I left Ursula and the kids three days later, and drove back to Washington to finish school.

I graduated from college 16 days later, and then went back to Winston-Salem, to join my family.

I was a civilian again, and we started a new life.

Following are two stories about one of my jobs in Washington.

Just a Dummy
Suitland, Maryland – 1959

At OSI District 4, I was assigned duty as the assistant to the District Training Officer and we developed a great training program for the special agents. We built crime scenes, which the special agents processed, to simulate what they did when they worked in the field.

At one point, we conducted some serious training on how to photograph crime scenes. The purpose of the training was to teach the Agents how to locate evidence, photograph it, and write a report about what they saw. Of course, any good crime scene had to have a dead person in it and we had mannequins that we could have used, but we decided that it would be better to use a live person posing as a murder victim. Guess who got the job of being the murder victim.

I put on my Air Force uniform and was made up to simulate a crime victim with a smashed skull, complete with blood and brains oozing out of the side of my head.

Then, I laid on the floor in the auditorium, facedown, with my arms and legs spread out, and with my eyes wide open. When the agents came in for the training session, most of them, at first, thought they were looking at a real corpse. For about four hours, I lay there, perfectly still, with very shallow breathing, while the agents took their pictures.

When the training session was over, I staggered to my feet amid applause from the agents. My right cheekbone, where it had been touching the floor, had a black and blue bruise mark, the size of a silver dollar, and my pelvic bone was so sore that I could hardly touch it. My knees were nearly paralyzed and the insides of my knees were badly bruised. It took several days for the bruises to disappear. It was a great experience.

Spooked
Suitland, Maryland – 1959

To set the scene for this story, I must describe the building in which DO 4 had its offices. It was a two-story, L-shaped, World War II vintage building, made of cheap lumber and covered with slate siding. It was cold and drafty in the winter, and hot in the summer. The whole building shook when the wind blew and the floors squeaked when walked upon. But despite its poor condition, the building was physically secure. The only doors that allowed entrance to the building were through the front lobby, where our security people always checked the credentials anyone who entered.

During off-duty hours a Special Agent was stationed at the door. He kept a log of who was in the building during off-duty hours. He also handled any calls that might come in during the night, and passed on important information to the proper people. In his desk drawer was a .38 caliber Policeman Special.

One of the methods of keeping the Special Agents well trained in their profession was to conduct simulated case drills, to see if they could solve the cases. One way to do this was to set up a crime scene, as realistic as we could make it, usually based on a real murder or robbery. We planted fingerprints, footprints, blood, bits of clothing, and any other clues that would help to solve a real case. Then, each day, a team of four agents "processed" the scene to look for clues, to find and identify all evidence. As they discovered the evidence, they photographed the scene and wrote a report on what they found.

Inside of a large room on the second floor, we constructed a room, made up of moveable walls, including windows, doors, etc., to simulate a room within a house.

During one such training session, we built a scene, based upon a real case, where a young woman had been raped and murdered in her barracks room. The attack had been especially brutal and it was easy to develop a crime scene with a great deal of evidence. We set up a typical barracks single room, dressed a manikin in a WAF uniform, and then tore up the room to simulate a struggle. We placed the manikin on the floor. Her clothes were torn and bloody, and her panties were ripped apart and laying on the floor next to her body. You get the picture. It was pretty gory. We planted evidence all over the place, and then left it for the agents to process the next day. We didn't tell anyone what we had done because we wanted to see the reaction of the agents when they first came upon the scene the next day.

It was about 11:00 PM and the duty agent was getting ready to go to bed, in an adjoining room. The only other person in the building was a janitor. The night was windy and the building shook slightly.

The janitor, a sixty-something year old man, was cleaning the last rooms in the far corner of the building. He opened the door to the training room and walked in, dust mop in hand. He dusted the floor around the fake room containing the crime scene. Then he happened to look through a window and saw the manikin.

The duty agent was brought to his feet by a terrifying scream.

He then heard the thump of running feet, headed in his direction. He looked out of his room to see the old man stumbling down the stairs. The man looked terribly frightened.

"There's a dead woman up there," he screamed, waving his arm in the general direction of the training room. "She's all bloody and tore up and she's dead," he stammered. He shuffled his feet and waved his arms. He was shaking so badly that he could hardly stay in one place.

That was one time that everybody was lucky that an experienced agent was on duty. The first reaction of most people would have been to call the police and ask questions later, but Special Agent Joe Thomas was too experienced to panic at the sight of a murder. After a few minutes, the old man had calmed down some and Joe, pistol in hand, went upstairs to check out the situation. The old man was a bit reluctant to go back up the stairs, but Joe insisted, so he went along.

When Agent Thomas realized the circumstances, he felt both anger and relief. He was mad at us for setting up the scene and for not telling him about it, but relieved that no one was injured. He explained the situation to the old man and sent him home. Then he called the Training Officer, at home, and gave him hell for scaring the old man so badly. Then he went to bed.

The next morning, the story spread, and everyone had quite a laugh about it. It made the training more enjoyable, knowing what had happened. Most of the teams found most of the evidence that we had planted. It was a very successful session, but after that, we always told the duty agent about any new crime scenes that we had set up.

Chapter 13

WINSTON-SALEM, NORTH CAROLINA – 1967-85

I was reunited with my family late Saturday afternoon, and on Monday morning I went to work as a technical writer at the Western Electric Company, Reynolda Road facility, an office building containing about 300 technical writers, engineers, and support personnel.

We lived in a rental house for only a month and then we decided to invest in a house in Davidson County, about 10 miles south of Winston-Salem. I purchased the house with a loan from the Veterans Administration, using what was called the World War II G.I. Bill of Rights. It was the first house that we had ever owned.

After just a few months of civilian life, my health began to fail. I became very nervous, couldn't sleep very well, and just got to where I was concerned about what was going on. I couldn't understand why I was getting paid so much money and doing so little work. After all those years in the Air Force, with the long hours, constant stress, and low pay, it didn't seem possible that I was working only 40 hours a week and was making more than twice as much money as I had in the Air Force. I began to doubt my ability and was afraid that this good job could not possibly be real.

I started getting headaches, had an upset stomach, and began feeling very tired all of the time. I contacted a local doctor, and after several visits, over several months, with complaints about various things, he said, "I just can't do anything more for you. I want to refer you to a psychiatrist." So he gave me a name, and the first thing that the psychiatrist said, after I told him my story, was that I had clinical depression. He prescribed some antidepressant pills, warned me that it would take a few days for the pills to take effect, and I went back to work.

The visit to the doctor was on the Thursday before Labor Day 1968, and over the Labor Day weekend I lost it. I went into deep depression and didn't know if I was going to live or die. On Monday morning I called the psychiatrist and he had me admitted to the psychiatric ward of Forsyth Memorial Hospital in Winston-Salem. I was in the hospital for 12 days, but I don't remember much about the first three or four days because I slept most of the time. I was under no restraints, except that I couldn't leave the ward.

They fed me well, and the staff was just wonderful. As you can imagine, it wasn't a very pleasant place to be, with everyone at least as sick I was, and some of them much worse. I wasn't allowed any visitors for the first week, then Ursula came and took me out to lunch and I began to feel better. Obviously the medicine had taken effect, and my condition was improving.

One evening I was standing in the back of the recreation room while several people were watching Billy Graham on television. He was preaching an evangelistic sermon, just like he always did, and I began to listen. I stayed and listened to him until he finished, and that night, for the first time in my life, **I prayed to God for help**. I felt a warm glow come over me, and for the first time in many months I began to relax. That was the beginning of my healing process, a process that has continued to this very day. And so, after 12 days in the hospital I was discharged and I went back to work. I was a bit rocky for a month or so but then, everything was back to normal.

I stayed on the medicine for about nine months, and then I told the doctor that I was going to make it on my own and that I was no longer going to take the medicine. He cautioned me that I might get sick again, but I thanked him for all that he had done, and I left his office. For many months, I went through periods of minor depression, but I learned to live with it and kept on going.

I have been on some sort of anti-depression medication, off and on, ever since.

The situation described above appears to be similar to what the military now call "Post-Trauma Stress Disorder (PTSD). I haven't discussed this with any veteran's doctors, but my situation; Constant stress, long working hours, school three nights a week and several part-time jobs, could have triggered a depression condition that I had for about a year before I retired. I hadn't asked for medical treatment because I was afraid that they wouldn't let me retire. Too much was at stake to stay any longer.

After I was released from the hospital I also realized that living so far out in the country, and driving so far to work every day, was becoming very difficult. Through the same real estate agent that had sold us the house in Davidson County, we arranged to buy a house, just being built in the Gordon Manor section of Winston-Salem, only a few miles from where I worked. The move really helped. Everything leveled off for me, and soon I was back to where the world looked bright again.

Shortly after moving back into town, we began attending Burkhead United Methodist Church and before long we became members. The following June, the church got a new Minister, the Rev. Donald Haynes, one of the finest men I've ever known. Within just a few months he asked me to serve on the Administrative Board as Chairman of Social Concerns, and I accepted the position.

For the next four years I worked with the Experiment in Self-Reliance, and other agencies, that provided services to the poor and needy in Forsyth County. In those four years I touched the lives of over 400 people, helping them with whatever problems they had. I visited them in their homes, bought groceries and medicine for them, and one Christmas I delivered nearly 100 Christmas presents to several families throughout the county. Whenever I needed money to help someone, Rev. Haynes spent a few minutes on Sunday morning explaining the need, and telling the people that if they could contribute to the cause, that they should see me after the service. Every time he did that, when I stood up, I was surrounded by people, handing me money.

Some days I left the church with several hundred dollars. I didn't keep track of the exact amount of money that I gathered or how I spent it, but I do know that I paid for a lot of medicine, bought a lot of groceries, and spent a lot of time, sometimes late at night, in the homes of people who needed help.

And, so it went, for four years and beyond. God has a wonderful way of putting the right person in the right place to help His people. It was some of the most rewarding years of my life, but I began to burn out, so I asked to be relieved from the job.

My family remained active in the church from then on. Ursula sang in the choir, I taught adult Sunday school, and our three children were active in the youth programs. During the following years, I organized the Methodist Men's Club, formed a Boy Scout troop, and constantly worked within the church.

Sometimes a person must hit the bottom before he can understand God. I have had a working relationship with Him ever since. My life was changed forever on that day that I watched Billy Graham on television in Forsyth Memorial Hospital.

In May 1972, we decided that since our children were growing up, we needed some more space, so we sold our house in Gordon Manner and bought a larger house on Weymouth Rd, on the west side of Winston-Salem. We lived in that house until I was transferred to Naperville, Illinois in 1985.

Now back to my work.

Even though I was hired as a technical writer, for the first five years with Western Electric, my job was that of a project planner in the engineering department of the Safeguard Missile Project, a US Department of Defense project.

There is a bit of a story about this assignment. When I was interviewed for the Western Electric job, I was interviewed by W. D. (Bill) Hawkins, the head of the Engineering Department, so when I arrived, he asked that I be assigned to his department.

That went well until, in the summer of 1972, the company wage practices people decided that I could no longer be assigned in Engineering and retain my rating as a Technical Writer. The rules were that, to work in engineering, a person had to have a Bachelor of Science in Electrical Engineering, and my degree was an Associate Degree (3 year) in Electronic Engineering. They wanted to reclassify me and transfer me to an administrative position.

At about the same time, the government cancelled the Safeguard Project, so all of that work was cancelled, and the writers were assigned to departments preparing the operations and maintenance manuals for the Bell telephone companies. Bill Hawkins took over a writing department and had me transferred to his department.

This is how the writing system worked:

The technical writers learned about the operations and maintenance of equipment by studying engineering drawings and from interviews with the design scientists at Bell Laboratories. Then they wrote the draft of a manual, using pencil and paper, and sent it to a group of editors, who checked it to be sure that it was properly composed. When the editor was finished with the draft, it was sent to the typing pool, and then the finished product was sent to the print shop for printing and distribution.

Most of the people that worked around me simply didn't understand how I did my job. Most of them took the engineering drawings, spread them out, studied them, and then, little by little, wrote the manual. I was a little different. I taped the drawings to the walls of my cubicle, stared at them for a few days, until I figured out how the machine worked, then picked up my pad and pencil and wrote the document, with only casual glances back to the drawings. Nobody said anything about it, but I think they thought I was a bit odd.

An interesting side to this story is that we were required to do our writing with a pad and pencil, and I was accustomed to working with a typewriter. I asked for a typewriter, but my request was denied. The system was set up the way it was, and no one would change it.

The work was always challenging and I had the opportunity to work with a great group of people. I traveled quite a bit, going to various Bell Laboratories locations and to telephone companies located all over the country.

After nearly ten years of engineering and writing assignments, on October 1, 1977, I was promoted to Task Group Leader, a first level management position, similar to that of a Section Chief. I did very little writing after that.

The position of Task Group Leader was quite a change for me. Instead of pouring over engineering drawings, and writing documents, I became a project planner and supervised about 10 technical writers; making writing assignments, checking their work, and maintaining discipline. For three years, my groups prepared manuals for use with electronic switching systems, then for seven years, for computer hardware and software.

At one point I was assigned to a new Task Group that was formed to evaluate some writers, from several departments, who had dropped to the bottom of the performance scale, and were being considered for dismissal. To make a long story short, in less than a year, out of the 10 men assigned to me, four of them resigned, and five of them raised their proficiency levels enough to be returned to normal assignments. The tenth one had apparently been mismanaged in his previous assignment, and after several months of observation, he was transferred to another department, where he was subsequently promoted to Task Group Leader. So my little experimental task group was dissolved, and I went on to other assignments.

In early 1985, Western Electric formed a new satellite department at Indian Hill Laboratories in Naperville, Illinois, just west of Chicago. The job was to assist Bell Labs in the technical writing activities being done, for them, by our group in Winston-Salem,

For several years I had wanted to get back up north, so I volunteered to take a position as Task Group Leader in that new department. When the department was formed, the new Department Chief was promoted from an assignment in a liaison group and had very little supervisory experience, even though he knew a lot of the management people in the Labs. He needed some help getting started, so I was transferred there as one of two Task Group Leaders that were to help him run the department. We sold our house in Winston-Salem, bought a condo in Naperville, and moved north. By then, our children were grown, so they stayed in the South.

Following are some stories about my life in Winston-Salem.

Black and Gold
Forsyth County, North Carolina – 1969-73

Her skin was dark brown and her heart was of pure gold.

I first met Inez while she was a case worker for the Experiment in Self Reliance (ESR), and I was doing some church work through that agency. She had been in the "welfare" business for many years, and knew all of the tricks of the trade. She knew where all available charity funds were and how to go about shaking them loose. She knew all of the charity-minded merchants in town, and knew just how much she could expect to get from each of them. She knew who was dealing in what and how to get the best deal for whatever she wanted.

If she couldn't find funds, she used her own.

She also knew all of the shady characters on the fringe of the ghetto. She knew the loan sharks, the used appliance and furniture dealers, the crooked automobile dealers, and the drink house operators. She knew how they operated and, in many cases she had caught them cheating the destitute ghetto people. She didn't call the law; she simply used the information to solicit "volunteers" for her projects.

She was one of the most interesting and dedicated persons that I've ever known.

This story is about Inez and how she helped Mary Jane Beck, a twelve year old leukemia victim that I was working with in my church ministry. Mary Jane and her mother were absolutely destitute. They lived on a small welfare check, nothing else. I worked with them for over three years, trying to keep their heads above water.

On one of my weekly visits to Mary Jane and her mother, I discovered a desperate situation. The kerosene stove that heated the house had quit working and the temperature in the house was near freezing.

On the Tuesday preceding my Saturday visit, the old stove had quit and Mrs. Beck had walked to a used appliance store to see if she could find another stove. The only money she had was her $96 welfare check. She found a kerosene stove that would fit her needs, and the manager sold it to her for exactly $96.00, delivered. Mrs. Beck filled the stove tank with kerosene and the house was warm again. There was no money for groceries, but at least little Mary Jane would be warm.

After only three days, the fan motor on the stove went dead and the stove was worthless. She called the store manager to complain, but was told that the best he could do was to sell her another used stove for $100.00. Of course, she didn't have the hundred dollars, so they were living without heat. They still had no groceries.

I checked the stove to verify that the motor was indeed burned out and that nothing could be done to fix it except to replace the motor. I knew that was not a practical solution.

For several minutes I pondered what to do, and then I remembered Inez and her connections. I called her at home. (Remember, this all happened on a Saturday.)

When I told her the problem, she asked me the name of the merchant who had sold the stove to Mrs. Beck. I told her his name.

"Why, that rotten bum," she shouted, "I've got enough on that guy to send him up for twenty years. Let me see what I can do."

I hung up the phone and waited. About thirty minutes later she called back.

She was laughing. "I made him an offer he couldn't refuse." she chuckled, "You'll have a stove before supper time. Let me know if you need anything else." I thanked her and hung up.

In less than an hour a stove was delivered and installed. The man that delivered it was very courteous.

The stove was still working fine the last time I visited the Beck family, over a year later.

Inez is gone now but I'll bet that if any of those scheming rascals made it to heaven, she is keeping them honest. What a wonderful person she was.

The last time that I heard from Mary Jane she was 18 years old and she called me to invite me to her wedding.

Footnote: Inez had a college degree and her husband was a college professor. They had put three children through college. She drove around in an old Chevy, which was full of stuff that she gave to the needy. She never told me where she got her supplies.

Birthday Party
Winston-Salem, North Carolina   1970

For Christmas 1971, our Social Concerns group came up with a fairly large project to help needy families. A few days before Christmas I delivered the presents that had been contributed by members of the church.

It was a birthday party in honor of a man named Jesus and it was the giving of gifts that the members of a church called Burkhead United Methodist had donated to the needy people of the county. It was the nicest birthday party that I've ever attended. I've been to parties of this type before but none quite so meaningful, none so large, and certainly none that will be so well remembered.

It all began over a month before Christmas when the Council on Ministries recommended that the Sunday School classes be offered the opportunity to sponsor a needy family for Christmas. During the weeks that followed, the classes gathered gifts, food, clothing, and money, and on a cold and rainy day the Thursday before Christmas, I set about delivering the load of goods to the families.

Doris and Jack, of the Experiment in Self-Reliance (ESR) and I met at the church at 9:00 A.M. and began to load up. Doris had been with ESR for over five years and was an old friend. We had worked together before. Her companion was new with the agency, had put in a tour in Vietnam, and tried college for a while before taking the job. As we loaded the gifts into the International Van, I joked about the 4-wheel drive vehicle, and Doris replied, "You'll be glad we have it before we're done today," and looked at me with a mischievous grin.

We finished loading and drove north, out into open farm country. After several miles we stopped at the first house of the sixteen that we were to visit that day.

The house was small and rundown. The woman of the house was small, thin, and 22. She met us at the door wearing what once had been a housecoat and Doris teased her about sleeping so late. Her smile was genuine but the missing teeth ruined the affect. As I entered the house, I was met by the odor of fuel oil, a smell that I have learned to associate with poverty. Two small, blond, boys popped in from another room and grinned at us, as only small boys can, and the place seemed a little less gloomy. We brought in the gifts, chatted for a few minutes and left.

As we wished the woman a Merry Christmas, she lisped, "It will be now," and tried to smile through the mist in her eyes.

We drove on through the rain.

The next stop was at the home of an elderly couple living in the worst filth that I had encountered in years. Jack and I entered the living room and were nearly blasted out by the heat from an old oil-burner, just inside the door. The room was stacked high with old furniture, newspapers, housewares, and junk. A man was sprawled on a ragged sofa watching a soap opera on a black and white TV, which was wedged into one corner of the room. He sat up, held his stomach with both hands, and talked to Jack about a doctor's appointment that had been made for him. He didn't seem to care if he saw the doctor or not. The woman only stood and listened. Jack gave them a small bag of fruit and cookies and we left. Doris told me that the man was a former share cropper, now too old and too ill to work. They were on welfare.

We left the main road and stopped at the entrance to what looked like a logging trail. Jack kicked the International into 4-wheel drive and we started up the trail. To reach the home on the hillside we churned for two miles through the woods, all four wheels grabbing for each foot of sticky, red clay The family was young, the children totaled four, ranging in age from eight months to ten years. The shack was something straight out of the comic strip, "Snuffy Smith," perched on the side of a hill, with no plumbing and no paint. A pair of electrical wires connected the house to the civilized world. The water supply was a spring, 300 yards down the hill and across a muddy creek. The woman told us that she was glad it was raining so she could catch rain water for washing and wouldn't have to carry it. We unloaded a large load of gifts. The woman couldn't believe her eyes. She was very grateful but couldn't understand why anyone would help her that way. The children were forcefully held away from the gifts while they were locked in an old car in the yard, the only place with a lock to keep them safe. The father was working at his construction job and wasn't at home.

A few miles further on we drove up to a large, old, two-story house looking down on a yard littered with dozens of junked cars. We walked into the house and entered a different world. In that house were nine of the most beautiful children I've ever seen. One little, redheaded, boy reminded me of a neighbor child of years gone by. They were all around us, laughing as I brought in the Christmas tree that the 6th grade Sunday School class had decorated. The older children and the mother beamed as we unloaded the gifts and the food. The father was in jail but would be home in a few weeks. I suppose that they'll never have much in material things but there was a whole lot of love in that house.

And so it went all day. Some were young families with skills that wouldn't raise them above the poverty level and some were elderly or too crippled or too feeble to help themselves. Each with a faint smile at seeing friends, each given some gifts, each responding to our "Merry Christmas" with an attempt to smile but knowing that there were no "Merry" Christmases for them anymore.

As we finished our deliveries and headed back to town, we stopped at the unpainted shack of a family recently burned out and not yet recovered. We gave them some clothes and a brand new $50 bill. The woman said that some of the money would be used to take her sick kids to the doctor.

The last stop of the day was at a house that we had been to before. Several months before, their kitchen stove had blown up and one of our church members had donated a stove to replace it. The father had had lung cancer for over three years and one of the daughters had sleeping sickness. They had been evicted from their trailer home and they had made do with what little furniture that could be found for them. The miracle of it all was the wonderful attitude of that family. They welcomed us, laughed with us, and could hardly wait to show us the day-old puppies of their dog, Doris. (My friend, Doris, looked over at me and grinned.) The man joked with us about the chewing tobacco we brought him because he had no teeth and would have to "gum" the tobacco. As we left, Doris told me that this would probably be his last Christmas. He was 45 years old. With all of that tragedy, they had a love and affection seldom seen in our fast moving society.

And so the birthday party came to an end as all parties must. The party was in celebration of the birth of our Lord and I believe that He was proud to be a part of it. As a Christian, I believe that God means for us to celebrate the birth of His son in this way and I'm sure that He is proud of us, as members of His church.

Big Man
Winston-Salem, North Carolina – 1971

Martha was a fifty year old woman who lived in a rented, three-room house with no heat and no furniture. Living with her was her twenty-four year old, mildly retarded daughter, and her four year old granddaughter. They were sleeping on the floor, on pallets made of old blankets. A few weeks before we found her, she had lost her job in Kernersville and had been evicted from a rented, furnished, house trailer.

The lady had two slipped disks in her back and was under the care of a doctor for cancer. When she smiled, you could sense the hurt.

To support her family, she had opened a small hamburger grill about a block from where she lived. It was in the small-industry part of town, so business was quite good. The grill was her only source of income.

We went to work on the project. We solicited the strong backs from some alcoholics at the Rescue Mission, and began to furnish the house. Church members donated three beds for Martha, her daughter and her granddaughter. (One of the beds came from the parsonage.) We located a used electric range and a Sunday School class bought it for her. Someone donated a sofa and someone else a television set. We obtained linens, clothing, silverware, and dishes. The place began to resemble a home, not just a house.

One of the items donated by a family in the church was a lovely, black, leather chair with a straight back and leather- covered arms. I brought the chair into the house and placed it in the living room. Martha immediately went to the chair and sat down. In a couple of minutes, she began to smile.

"This chair is the best gift of all," she said, "It's just perfect for my back. Now I can rest without hurtin' so much."

One evening, a few weeks later, I went to visit Martha to see how she was getting along and when I arrived, I found her sitting in her favorite chair; crying. When I asked what the trouble was, she told me that a man from the tax office had come to the grill and had advised her that unless the back-taxes on the property were paid, the grill would be closed. She had been unable to convince the man that she had not been in the building the year before, therefore could not possibly owe the taxes. She had come home from work that evening terribly upset, for after all, if she lost the grill she would lose her ability to support her family. She was very proud of the fact that she didn't receive welfare and was able to take care of herself and her family without help from the government.

I sat down on the sofa and talked to her for over an hour, until she began to feel better. I gave her the phone number of the Legal Aid Society and suggested that she call them the next day to see if they could help. I stood up to leave and as I reached the door, I turned to look back to where she was still sitting in that lovely old chair. I felt very helpless.

"I'm sorry that I'm not big enough to help you," I said, "If I could, I'd go down to city hall and talk to them myself, but it wouldn't do any good."

She looked up at me and a tear rolled down her left cheek. She said, "Mister Monson, you're a pretty big man to me."

Now, I must tell you that I left her house rather suddenly. I tried to smile and failed. I said a quick, "Thank you," then fled. I didn't want her to see a grown man cry.

There I was, a man who had been fighting for his life, against depression, only a few years before, a person who had given up hope of ever leading a normal life again, and here was a woman who was hurting so badly that she probably wanted to die, but yet she had just call me a "big man." I dashed to my car and drove home.

There is no way that I can measure that experience in terms of medicinal value. It was too much.

Depressed
Winston-Salem, North Carolina – 1972

Judy came to us by a round-about sort of way. She had been living in Arizona with her husband and two children, but she had gotten depressed, and her husband had her committed to a mental hospital. She stayed in the hospital only a week, and then she walked away and came to Winston-Salem to live with her sister. After only three weeks, her sister had thrown her out. She asked the Department of Social Services for help and the case worker called me.

We called the hospital in Arizona and determined that they weren't looking for her and didn't want to bring her back. They confirmed that her illness was depression and that she was of no danger to anyone but herself. But she did have a problem. She couldn't go back to Arizona, and her family here didn't want her either. We decided to help.

Within our church was a lovely lady named Mary Jones, who volunteered to coordinate the project. So, under the direction of Mary, and with the help of a good many very fine people in the church and in the neighborhood, we found her an apartment and raised enough money to pay the rent and to buy a few things to get her started. Mary helped her decorate the apartment, made some curtains, and did some painting. In short, she did those wonderful things that make a house into a home. It was not long before we could see a decided improvement in Judy's outlook on life.

She enrolled in Forsyth Technical Institute, found a job, and was soon on her way to recovery. She started coming to church regularly and many of the congregation got to know her. We could notice a steady improvement in Judy's condition and we were truly overjoyed at the progress.

After a few months, she decided that she was feeling well enough to go back to her family. So, with money from her new friends, she went back to her husband and her children in Arizona.

Several months later I received a letter from a man in Arizona who was interested in employing Judy and asking for a character reference. I wrote back and told him how much we loved Judy and recommended her for the job. That was the last that I heard of her. I hope that she is doing well.

Rewards
Winston-Salem, North Carolina – 1973

I was working with Don Haynes, our Minister, one weekend, at a retreat for the church confirmation class. It was a peaceful evening and we were sitting around a lodge fire at Tanglewood Park. Don was telling the children about some of the work that the church did, and he asked me to relate some of my experiences in social work.

I spent about an hour explaining to them how it was done and telling some of the stories similar to the ones that I have told here. I also related to them what it meant to me to be part of a program for helping people.

Two weeks later, Janice, the mother of one of the twelve-year-olds, stopped me after church and related a most interesting story.

She stated that the night before, she and her daughter, Laurie, had been discussing Laurie's future. When asked what she wanted to do when she became older, Laurie replied, "I want to be like Mister Monson; he helps people."

Rewards are not necessarily monetary.

There's a lesson here for anybody who has never been involved with helping the less fortunate people of our society. There's no way that I can measure what this activity did for me. The memories of my depression and the recovery from it were constantly in my thoughts and I felt a strong need to help others survive from their problems. I found that, as I helped others, I was helping myself come out of the pit that I had been in for so long. There are many agencies that provide these services and they need all the help they can get. Give it a try; you'll be glad you did.

Shot Down
WINSTON-SALEM, NORTH CAROLINA – 1983

Conrad Blalock was a genuine Carolina country boy. He was born here, raised here, and except for military service in World War II, never left the state for more than two weeks. He was slow moving, friendly, and the most likeable cuss you would ever want to meet. We worked together as technical writers at Western Electric in the 1970s and I got to know him quite well.

The story that I am about to tell was developed over several years of friendship and through many conversations. He didn't discuss his wartime experiences freely because he was concerned that somebody might think of him as a "hero."

In the summer of 1943, Conrad was drafted into the Army Air Corps and sent to pilot training. He had a feeling that driving an airplane was not for him, but he did as he was told. He lasted three weeks and washed out, then became a bombardier instead of a pilot.

After graduation from bombardier school he was sent to England and began flying combat missions over France and Germany with the 8th Air Force. On his fourteenth mission, his B-17 was hit by ground fire over France and started to go down. The pilot ordered the crew to bail out. The pilot managed to stabilize the airplane and, with two wounded crewmen, made it back to England.

Conrad landed in a turnip patch with a broken left leg and a dislocated left shoulder. He was untangling himself from his chute when he realized that he was surrounded by French civilians carrying pitchforks and clubs. His captors took him to a nearby farm house, patched him up as best they could, and turned him over to the French Resistance. He lived with partisans of the French Underground for the next six months.

The first priority was to heal his broken bones. He was placed with a farm family where he remained hidden in the attic until his leg and shoulder healed sufficiently for him to travel. During that time the farmhouse was searched repeatedly by German soldiers, but his tiny cubicle behind the chimney in the attic was never discovered. That same hiding place was used by dozens of American and British fliers throughout the war. Discovery would have meant death for the farmer and his family.

After about four months, Conrad was well enough to travel and the long trek to freedom began.

From Normandy to Paris he traveled by foot and by farmer's cart, posing as the retarded, deaf-mute, son of a peasant farmer who was actually a Resistance fighter. After nearly a day in Paris, they boarded a train for southern France. During that day in the Paris train station, Conrad and his "father" sat on a bench in the railroad station, with German troops all around them. They were questioned several times but were not detected for what they were.

In the Pyrenees Mountains, near the French-Spanish border, they were met by Spanish Communist guerrillas who were helping the Allies smuggle downed airmen out of France and across Spain to Gibraltar.

As soon as Conrad was turned over to the guerrillas, the French farmer returned home. Conrad was taken to a camp in the mountains and stayed there until joined by eleven other downed fliers.

From that moment until they reached the safety of Gibraltar, the fliers were under the iron fist of five heavily armed Spanish guerrillas. Each day they traveled over a hidden route, seldom seeing any other persons. At night they slept in abandoned shepherd's cabins. They ate only cold food. No smoking or fires were allowed. The guerrillas were risking their lives to save the fliers and they allowed no actions that would jeopardize their mission or their safety.

On the evening of the third day, a young American officer began complaining. He said that they were going too fast, and that his feet hurt. He complained about the food, about the sleeping conditions; about everything. The next morning he announced that he would go no farther and would stay there until his feet got better and another group came along. The guerrillas simply ignored him and moved the rest of the group up the mountain. An hour after breaking camp, one of the guerrillas left the group under the guise of a scouting mission. Two hours later he reappeared and the march proceeded. The young officer was never seen again.

Conrad said that the man was probably killed because it was too dangerous to leave him behind. If he was captured by persons sympathetic to the Germans, he could have been forced to tell them about the entire underground operations, thereby endangering the lives of all of the airmen being rescued and the people who helped them.

It took nearly a month for the group to cross Spain and enter Gibraltar. They were flown back to England, over water all the way, and the Americans were returned to the United States. Downed fliers were never returned to combat. They knew too much about the escape routes and the French Resistance.

All through the years after the war, Conrad corresponded with the family that had hidden him, and about 30 years ago, they came to Carolina to visit him.

Conrad died about 20 years ago of complications from a compound fracture of his left ankle. His body was too weak to fight off the infection caused by the break.

Wooden Leg
Winston-Salem, North Carolina – 1984

Bill Herman had his right leg amputated mid-thigh during the Korean War. The Army gave him a new leg, he learned to use it, and then he came home. He went to college, earned an engineering degree in three years, and then went to work in his profession. He was one of the best technical people I knew during my time at Western Electric Company

When I first met Bill, he was about forty years old. He had never been married.

But Bill had a problem; women wouldn't leave him alone. Everywhere he went, women sought him out. A trip to a bar, any bar, and he was set for the evening. Frankly, I was envious of him, but at times I feared for his health; he looked so tired.

I never could figure out why he was so popular. He was not handsome; he was not even a good physical specimen. He stood about five feet seven and weighed at least 175 pounds. Numerous cases of beer had settled around his waist. His brown, straight, hair was turning to skin in the center. He had a rather large nose, pushed slightly to the left.

And it couldn't have been his money, because he didn't have any. He spent it as fast as he made it.

So the mystery remained. He simply had some hidden talent that I never figured out.

One of Bill's favorite companions was a young lady named Betty Hall. Betty was a twenty-five year old brunette, five-foot-three, dainty, and very sexy. She had her pick of the bachelors, and a few married men, but she chose Bill.

They had a very unique arrangement. They both dated other people, but if either felt a spur-of-the-moment need for companionship, a phone call brought them together. It seemed like an ideal setup. Both were very active on the social scene, but whenever either needed the other, they got together.

This had been going on for several years when Bill met Hilda Marshall. To say he fell in love is to put it a bit too strongly. What he did was, sort of, fell in "like." Well, let's just say, he liked her performance.

Hilda was more Bill's type than Betty was. She was nearly forty, a bit wide across the rump, but very neat and really quite attractive. She had been married and divorced twice. She had decided to make Bill her third attempt at wedded bliss.

They dated for about six weeks, and then she moved in with him. He liked the idea. She was a good lover, and she even could cook a little. She was a lousy housekeeper, but Bill had lived alone all of his adult life, so he took care of the house work. They planned a September wedding.

But the tranquility didn't last. As the wedding day approached, they became more and more hostile toward each other. Neither of them could understand what was happening. They shrugged it off as pre-wedding jitters.

In an attempt to please his bride-to-be, Bill went to the pet store and laid out five hundred dollars for a six week old German-Shepherd male puppy. Hilda had mentioned several times that she wanted a watchdog to protector her, when he was out of town, so he bought the pup for her.

The dog was a beautiful little creature with a black face and ears that stood straight up. Hilda took him into the house and immediately made a lap-dog out of him. She never considered what would happen when he grew up. The dog naturally became very attached to Hilda, lying next to her on the sofa or in her lap every time she was in the room. He followed her around the house or out into the yard. They were inseparable. It was sort of cute - if you don't mind seeing a dog tear up good furniture.

The gift didn't help. The situation just got worse. They fought constantly. They no longer enjoyed each other's company. They threw things. If it hadn't been for the joy of making up after each fight, they wouldn't have stayed together as long as they did.

But finally, after nearly six months, the romance ended. They had a hell of a row over the dog. Bill insisted that the dog was Hilda's and that she should walk him but Hilda insisted that since Bill had bought the beast, that he should walk him. The argument had been going on for several days when it came to a head.

The dog had to go out. It was raining. He went into the kitchen where Hilda was preparing dinner, and nudged her leg with his nose.

Hilda retrieved the leash from behind the door, hooked it to the dog's collar, and started through the living room on her way to the front door. Bill was sitting in the recliner, reading the evening paper. Hilda opened the door and noticed the rain; she decided that she no longer owned a dog.

She dragged the dog over to Bill, handed him the leash, and returned to the kitchen. Without looking up, Bill took the leash and led the dog to the door. Then he also noticed the rain and figured out what was happening. He left the dog at the door and went into the kitchen.

The war began. The dog stood by the door, a pained expression on his face.

"What the hell's the matter with you," Bill asked, "Why don't you want to walk your friggin dog?"

"He's not <u>my</u> dog," Hilda screamed. "I'll be damned if I'll go out in the rain with him one more time. I'm tired of getting wet just so that damned dog can take a leak. Why don't you take him out once in a while?"

"I bought him for you, you bitch," Bill yelled, "Either you take care of your mutt or get your big fat ass out of my house. I've had about all I can take from you!"

"Well, that's all right with me," she snapped. "Give me five minutes and I'll be out of here." She spun on her heel and dashed upstairs. A few minutes later she came down, carrying her suitcase. Bill was standing in the middle of the room, contemplating the latest turn of events.

The dog still stood by the door, looking more pained than before.

As Hilda reached the door and opened it, Bill said, "What about the damned dog? He's yours. I laid out five hundred bucks for the mutt, the least you can do is take him with you."

"Not on your life," she replied, "You bought him, you keep him." She stomped out of the house, leaving the door open. She ran through the rain to her car, jumped in, and slammed the door.

Bill still stood in the middle of the room. He couldn't decide whether to laugh or to cry.

The dog looked out the door until Hilda's car drove away. Then, very casually, he walked over to where Bill was standing, raised his left leg, and squirted on Bill's wooden leg. When he was finished, he walked across the room, jumped up on the sofa, curled up, and went to sleep.

Bill went to the phone and called Betty Hall.

Chapter 14

NAPERVILLE, ILLINOIS – 1985-88

For the first couple of months, everything went very well. I slipped right into the routine of running the department; managing writers, giving briefings and presentations, and we were getting the department up and running quite well. I attended an unusual number of meetings with the Bell Labs people, just to brief them on what we were doing.

At first everything went well, but soon it seemed as if they didn't really want us there. Before long, a technical writing group was formed by Bell Labs, and, little by little, they began to cut into our business, appearing to want to take over all of the technical writing activities. I don't know what their motive was but I do know that our group was made up of writers with college degrees in electronic engineering and the writers that they were hiring had degrees in English. Apparently they didn't understand the qualifications of a technical writer.

So, we continued doing our work, knowing that to do technical writing we had to have the technical knowledge to fit the product. Because of those differences, a large division began to emerge between us and the Labs managers, and I was constantly disagreeing with someone within their organization.

As the pressures began to grow, my depression returned and I felt the stress building within my system. I felt that I couldn't continue butting heads with people all day and still keep my efficiency level up. I had over 19 years of service with the company, and would be eligible for retirement in less than a year, so I asked our management to reclassify me from Writing Supervisor to Technical Writer and to leave me on the job in that capacity until my retirement. They reluctantly approved my request and I became a Technical Writer, with no reduction in salary, but with no writing assignments. I did routine tasks for the Department Chief for a few months, and then put in my retirement papers.

All the time that I was at Bell Labs my personnel records were maintained at the Reynolda Road location, so my retirement was to be processed in North Carolina. I had about six weeks of leave time accrued, so when that was figured in, my retirement date was set for February 8, 1988. In mid-November of 1987, Ursula drove our car to Winston-Salem, and rented an apartment for us. The week before Thanksgiving I rented a U-Haul moving van, hired a couple of guys to help me load our furniture and our personal belongings, and then drove the truck to Winston-Salem. I flew back to Illinois, rented a room in a private home, sold the condo, worked until my leave time kicked in, and then drove back to Winston-Salem.

So now, at the age of 59, I was retired for the second time. I haven't drawn a paycheck since.

Chapter 15

REAL RETIREMENT – 1988-

We lived in the rented apartment for six months then bought a nice little cluster home in a community called Lantern Ridge. It was quite small but it had a master bedroom and two smaller bedrooms, plus a living room and an eat-in kitchen. There also was a two-car garage, just great for one car and a lot of storage. It was just right for us old, retired, folks.

It was great to have a place with no outside maintenance. When we wanted to travel we just locked the door and drove away.

Now we began to realize what retirement was all about. The last summer that we were in Illinois we had done some camping along the Mississippi River, using our Chevy van as a camper, but we had never been in a camping trailer or RV, so when we got back to North Carolina we went to a camper dealership to see what we could find. We didn't have much money to spend, so we ended up buying an old, beat up, trailer for a couple thousand dollars, and had a hitch put on the van.

We took a few short trips to campgrounds in the area, looked over some maps and then decided to try out a campground on Edisto Island, just south of Charleston, South Carolina. We had heard about Edisto from some friends in Naperville, Illinois and they told us that they were going to be at Edisto that weekend.

We loaded up the trailer and drove to Edisto, planning to spend a few days there as our first adventure as real campers. We pulled into the campground and rented a space, then found out that, somewhere along the line, I had scraped the rear end of the trailer on something, and had knocked a big hole in the wastewater holding tank. It was too late in the day to try and fix anything, so we slept in the trailer that night, and early the next morning we left the trailer on Edisto Island and went to Charleston to see if we could find some repair parts to fix the tank. We found a camper dealer, and when I explained the situation to him, he suggested that we trade the trailer for a used one that he had on the lot. We looked over the unit that he offered us, agreed to a price for the trade in, then jumped in the van, and drove back to Winston-Salem. We drew some money from our savings account and the next morning we drove back to Charleston. I took the old trailer to the dealership, and within an hour we had transferred our belongings from the old trailer to the new one, and headed back to Edisto Island. We set up the trailer and spent a beautiful weekend, eating fresh oysters cooked over an open fire.

We had arrived. We were now full-fledged campers and we were ready to go on with our retirement plans.

For several years, in addition to local trips, we took at least one six-week trip each year, either in the spring or the fall, just wandering. At one point, we upgraded both the trailer and the truck, but the pattern remained the same. We followed a pattern of activity that seemed to be just right for what we wanted to do. We got up in the morning, ate breakfast, then packed up the trailer, hitched it to the truck and leisurely drove along, stopping whenever we saw something that we wanted to look at. We very seldom traveled on the interstates, but stayed on the local roads, passing through a lot of wonderful little towns, and meeting some very nice people. As we traveled down the road, about 3 o'clock in the afternoon, we looked at our campground directory, found a place within a reasonable distance, went there, and set up the camper. We usually stayed at any given place for three nights, looking over the countryside, meeting the people and then moving on. We always had food in our gas-powered refrigerator, water in our freshwater tank, and a bathroom onboard, so we were totally independent. Life was good.

We took trips to Niagara Falls and Canada, to Florida, to New England, and one year we went all the way to North Dakota, with stops in Missouri and Minnesota.

The most memorable trip was to North Dakota. This was sort of a homecoming trip for me because we stopped in Minnesota and visited with many of my relatives, and then moved on to North Dakota, where we stopped at the farm where I had lived as a boy. We met and visited with the family that had bought the farm from my parents when we left there in 1937. When we had left the farm, these nice folks were only 26 years old, and they had lived there ever since we left. They told us that, about two years after we left, the house had burned down, and that they had rebuilt it on the same foundation. Most of the old farm buildings had been replaced, but the outhouse was still standing at the same place that it had been when I left. They told us that it came in handy when they had large family gatherings.

For a couple of years, everything went well, then, in the summer of 1990, while on a trip to Edisto Island, Ursula began having trouble breathing, and we decided that we should go home so she could see a doctor. She went through a series of tests and was diagnosed with a disease called "pulmonary hypertension," an incurable disease of the lungs. At first we were devastated, but then we decided that, with the help of an electric scooter, we could continue with our travels. We bought a scooter, installed a lift in the back of the truck, and we were ready to roll again.

We had to slow down a little bit, but sometimes it was quite humorous to see us old folks traveling like we did. One time, at Niagara Falls, she just about ran my legs off going up and down those hills near the Falls. We laughed a lot, especially when I had to tell her to slow down so I could keep up.

In November of 1991, we went to Florida, found a nice campground near Barstow, Florida, and rented a parking spot for six months. It was nice and warm and we thought it would be great to spend the whole winter just sitting in the sun.

But within less than a month, Ursula's breathing became more difficult, and we knew that we had to go home to see her doctor. So the week before Christmas, we left the trailer at Barstow, and drove home for Christmas. When she went to the doctor, he recommended that she not travel any more. In January, Carol's husband, Dallas, and I went to Florida and brought the trailer home. We had been living the good life for over three years.

Since we couldn't travel anymore, we decided to move to a house that was better equipped to handle our situation. Not only was Ursula in bad shape, but I had worked for 40 years, and I knew that if I didn't have something to keep me busy, I would have trouble with my depression again. We found a nice house, with a big back yard, on Remington Road, between Winston-Salem and Clemmons. We sold our house and moved.

The new house was a one story, three-bedroom house, with a game room and garage in the basement. The stairs to the basement were a problem, but we solved that by putting in a motor-driven "stair climber," to help Ursula get up and down the stairs.

Then I went to work in the back yard. The first thing that I built was a pear-shaped fishpond/lily pond, with a waterfall and fountain, and surrounded it with beautiful perennial flowers. Then I built a perennial flower garden, a rose garden, and a desert garden.

While I worked in the yard Ursula often came out onto the back deck to watch me work. She was on oxygen most of the time, but she was still able to do some of the cooking and light housework.

On August 2, 1992, the kids held a 40th anniversary party for Ursula and me at Burkhead United Methodist Church. We knew that Ursula wouldn't live to celebrate our 50th anniversary, so it was decided to celebrate our 40th instead. All of our friends were there and we had a grand time. Ursula was on oxygen by then and in a wheelchair most of the time, but she was very excited and received a record number of hugs that day.

In October 1992, I was mowing the lawn, when I felt a pain in my lower chest. I went to the doctor, they ran some tests, and found that I had blockages in five arteries leading to my heart, and I needed to have bypass surgery. All of this was discovered on a Friday, and on Monday I had surgery. I went into surgery about suppertime, and woke up about 6:30 the next morning. The surgery was a total success, and after seven days, I went home. During the surgery, Ursula, and all of our children, sat through the night in the waiting room. The ordeal took a lot out of Ursula, and she was so weak that she couldn't come to see me in the hospital. Carol stayed with her all the time that I was in the hospital.

I was pretty weak when I came home, but I didn't have time to feel sorry for myself. After several weeks, Carol and I agreed that she could go home, and I became a housekeeper and a caregiver.

Ursula got progressively weaker, and on August 8, 1993, with me at her bedside in the hospital, she died.

We had a beautiful memorial service at Burkhead United Methodist Church, and then her ashes were interred at Parklawn Cemetery.

Several years later her ashes were moved to the Columbarium at Clemmons United Methodist Church, in Clemmons, where I had become a member.

She was a wonderful wife and mother and it was a tough time for all of us, but we knew that she was with God, and that comforted us.

We had been married for 41 years and six days.

Chapter 16

OUR CHILDREN

As I mentioned earlier, Ursula and I had three children: Carol, Gary, and Adele. I hope that, at some future time, each of them will write their own story and I don't want to write their stories for them, but it seems appropriate to brag about them a little.

These children are the joy of my life and I'm very proud of them. They are all very independent and successful in their lives. They have learned that to be a whole person they must be proud, confident, resourceful, generous and courteous; and above all, to be willing to face their world in their own way. That's what I mean by "independent."

Each of them received as much education as they wanted to have, with very little help from their parents. All of them have had their ups and downs, and have handled each situation wisely. Even though they live far apart, they keep in close contact with each other, and their love and affection is always present.

Following is a brief description of each of our children, presented in the order of their birth.

Carol Jean

Born: August 8, 1958 in the American Hospital in Paris, France. Her birth was registered with the French government, but she is a native-born US citizen, based on the fact that Ursula and I were both US citizens at the time of her birth.

She married *Gary Lee Guyton* on December 17, 1976 at Burkhead United Methodist Church in Winston-Salem, North Carolina. Gary was killed in an automobile accident on May 8, 1978.

She married *William Dallas Carroll* on August 10, 1985 at Burkhead United Methodist Church, Winston-Salem, North Carolina.

They now live on their farm in Stokes County, near Danbury, North Carolina.

She has been employed as a legal assistant, by several attorneys, since she graduated from Reynolds High School in Winston-Salem, North Carolina.

Gary Christian

Born: October 25, 1960 in the Base Hospital, Andrews Air Force Base, Maryland.

He married *Julia Louise Rocci* on March 28, 1987, in Seneca, South Carolina. They now live in Simpsonville, South Carolina

He holds a bachelor's degree in electrical engineering from Clemson University and has been employed as an engineer since graduating from college.

Gary and Julie have three children:

Alexandra Louise, born July 7, 1988, in Greenville, South Carolina.

She currently lives at Fort Riley, Kansas, with her husband, US Army Staff Sergeant *R.C. Walton*. They have a son *Owen Richard Walton*, my first great-grandchild, born on July 6, 2014, in Seoul, South Korea.

Andrew Christian, born January 28, 1992, in Greenville, South Carolina.

He is currently serving in the U.S. Air Force at Moody Air Force Base, Georgia. He is married to *Mary Margaret Jacobson*, who is also serving in the Air Force. Mary is from Minnesota and is of Swedish descent. What a nice coincidence; Andrew married a Swede from Minnesota.

Katherine Ruth, born October 11, 1995, in Stockbridge, Georgia. She currently lives with her parents.

Adele Marie

Born: December 4, 1961, in the Base Hospital at Andrews Air Force Base, Maryland.

She married *Gregory Christian Jones* on July 31, 1982, at Burkhead United Methodist Church, Winston-Salem, North Carolina. - Divorced

They have a daughter, <u>*Lauren Ashley Jones*</u>, born October 7, 1985, in Forsyth Memorial Hospital, Winston-Salem, North Carolina.

Lauren currently lives in Winston-Salem, North Carolina. She recently graduated from Guilford Community College in Greensboro, North Carolina, and works as an Events Planner, at a convention center near Greensboro.

Adele married *George Verevkin* on December 31, 1991, in Winston-Salem, North Carolina. - Divorced

They have a daughter, <u>*Sophia Nicole Verevkin*</u>, born April 1, 1993 in Forsyth Memorial Hospital, Winston-Salem, North Carolina. She lives with her father and works at a restaurant in Winston Salem, North Carolina.

Adele married *Ross Cogar* on August 21, 2006 in Winston-Salem, North Carolina.

They currently live in Lebanon, Ohio.

Adele holds a bachelors degree in business administration from Gardner Webb University, Boiling Springs, North Carolina, and has worked in the banking industry for over 25 years.

Chapter 17

STARTING OVER – 1993

I went back to the empty house and, after feeling totally lost for a few days, I began to come back to life. I got busy in my gardens, visited with my kids and friends, and soon I began to feel better. A week or so later, I remembered that I had a life insurance policy, and now that I no longer needed to worry about supporting anyone after I was gone, I cashed in the insurance policy and bought a new Chrysler New Yorker. I'd never owned a luxury car before, so it was quite a treat for me to act like a big-shot. As my mother used to say, "Boys will be boys."

On the day of the funeral, I had received many sympathy cards, and when I got home I had tossed them on the kitchen counter, hoping to read them all when I had time. About six weeks later, I looked over at that pile of cards and there was a card from a friend of ours, Mary Jones, who had been a member of our church for many years and had sung in the church choir with Ursula. (You've already read about Mary Jones in one of the stories about my work in social work.) Mary had visited Ursula just a few days before she died. I picked up the card, read it, then called her and asked her if she would like to have dinner with me. She accepted my invitation and I entered into a new phase of my life.

Mary Jackson was born in Champaign, Illinois, on February 8, 1930. She graduated from the University of Illinois, with a degree in music education in 1952. She married Val Jones, an electrical engineer, who had graduated from Illinois two years earlier, and was then living in Buffalo, New York. They lived in Buffalo for a few years, and then moved to Owego, New York. In 1969 Val decided that he no longer wanted to be married and they were divorced. Mary and Val had three daughters, Lynn, Kathy, and Susan. After a couple years of part-time teaching, and of updating her education, she and her three girls moved to Winston-Salem, North Carolina in 1971, to be near her sister, Margo Jackson Crotts. Mary joined Burkhead United Methodist Church, and that's where we met. She worked for the Forsyth County school system for nearly 22 years, retiring in June 1994.

When I asked her to go to dinner, she asked me what time I would pick her up, and I said "5:00 o'clock." There was a slight pause, and then she said, "Okay." I had been retired for many years and was accustomed to eating early to avoid the crowds. It never occurred to me that she might not be able to leave work that early, but I guess she did, for when I got to her condo, she was ready to go. We had a very nice dinner at the Red Lobster, and then we went over to her condo and visited for a couple of hours. She showed me around her lovely home, and when we went down into the basement, the first thing that I noticed was, a fully-decorated Christmas tree, standing on a table, just as if it was waiting for Christmas. For some reason, it struck me as being funny, and for the first time in a long time I laughed. It sure felt good to laugh.

That first date was on September 10, 1993, and when she cooked dinner for me at her condo, a week later, I was hooked for life. We've been together ever since.

For the next couple of months we had a great time as we got to know each other better. We did all of the things that young folks do when they first start dating, such as eating out, going to movies, eating out, having picnics, going for long drives, and eating out. I was 64 years old and she was 62.

By mid-November, I was deeply in love. One evening at her home, as we were watching television, I suddenly got up from my chair, went over to her, got down on one knee, and asked her to marry me. She was a bit startled, but, after a bit of thought, she said, "Yes," and we began to make plans for our wedding.

It occurred to me that the Department of Internal Revenue would never understand how I could have had two wives in one year, so we set a tentative date of January 1, 1994 as our wedding day.

When we told our friends that we were getting married, we began to find out how many friends we really had. A few years before we got together, Mary had moved her membership from Burkhead United Methodist Church to the United Church of Christ, a church that her sister Margo, and her family, had attended for many years. So, we now had two church families, each of which had many people who wanted to come to our wedding. Add to that, Mary's Sweet Adelines Chorus, her teaching buddies, my former co-workers, and my Toastmasters Club, there was quite a crowd. We had a problem on our hands. It didn't seem practical to have a big church wedding, with a full reception, with all of those people. After all, at our age, we really didn't want to get too fancy, so we decided to elope. We also decided that, at a later date, when all of our children and grandchildren could attend, we would have a get-together and celebrate the occasion.

Our old friend, and former Pastor at Burkhead Church, Don Haynes, was living in Charlotte at the time, and we decided to ask him to perform our wedding service. So I called him and when I told him who I wanted to marry, his immediate reply was, "Mary is one of my favorite people, and I will be happy to perform the ceremony." We talked things over and he agreed to see if he could find a place to hold the ceremony. We agreed to the January 1st date, and after much searching, he came up with the Chapel in the Methodist Home (the senior citizens home) in Charlotte.

So, we went to Charlotte late in December, got our marriage license, and then on New Years Day, 1994, we met Don and his wife Joan, at the Chapel and we were married. Of course, to meet the requirements of the law, we had to have two witnesses; so Joan was one witness, and a janitor who just happened to walk by, was the other. As the ceremony was being performed, quite a few people, who lived in the Home, looked in and smiled.

The next morning, something happened that we have laughed about ever since. We had rented a room at one of the better hotels in downtown Charlotte, so we ate dinner in the hotel dining room, then went upstairs and went to bed. In the morning, about 6 o'clock, the clock radio came on very loudly, and I jumped out of bed, completely confused; in a strange room, with a strange woman. Apparently, whoever had last rented the room had set the alarm and hadn't turned it off.

So Mary went back to her work as a kindergarten teacher, and I went back to being retired. I moved some of my personal things into Mary's condo, and we began to search for a house that would be our new home.

God must have arranged for Mary to come into my life, because there is no other way that I can explain how I was so lucky as to marry such a wonderful woman to help me the rest of the way.

We looked at a lot of places, and then we bought a three bedroom, ranch style house, with a large yard, in Clemmons. Mary sold her condo and I sold my house, and we moved to Clemmons. The first thing that we did after we got moved in was to join the Clemmons United Methodist Church. We are still very active members there.

We had talked to our kids about our plans for a family celebration, and had decided to have the party in early April, when everybody could be there. We arranged for a large dining room in the Holiday Inn in Clemmons, and had a dinner, with all the trimmings. Every one of our children and their spouses and our grandchildren were there. What a wonderful time that was.

At the end of the school year, Mary retired and we were free to do anything we wanted to do. By combining our retirement incomes, we found that, if we were careful with our money, we could even take a few trips.

Since long before we were married, Mary's family had been having family reunions, every two or three years, and in July 1994 the reunion was to be held in California, near Lake Tahoe. We decided to make a "honeymoon" out of it and to drive to California and back, being tourists all the way. We were gone from home for about six weeks, and traveled over 10,000 miles. We went out the northern route, across Tennessee, Kentucky, and Indiana before stopping in Champaign, Illinois, to spend some time where Mary grew up. From there we went north, across Iowa, up to my old stomping grounds in southern Minnesota, where Mary got to meet many of my cousins. After a few days there we headed west, stopping at such places as, Mt. Rushmore and the Badlands of South Dakota, the Grand Tetons and Yellowstone Park in Colorado, Glacier National Park in Montana, Mt. St. Helens in Washington, Crater Lake in Oregon, Redwood National Park in northwestern California, and then stopped to visit Mary's brother Will, and his family, in Auburn, California. After a few days with Will, we went to the family reunion for a week, where I met dozens of members of Mary's family. What a great group they are. They immediately accepted me into the family and we have been very close ever since.

On the way back we traveled down the center of California, crossed the Mojave Desert, (115 degrees during the day), visited the Grand Canyon in Arizona, and the ancient Indian cliff dwellings at Mesa Verde in Colorado. While we were at the Indian dwellings, at about 12,000 feet above sea level, my heart-beat became irregular, and we had to interrupt our travels and head for the nearest medical facilities. It took us over four hours to get to an emergency room in Durango, Colorado. They checked me over, told me it was probably the high elevation that caused the problem and gave me a heart monitor to wear overnight. The next morning we went back to the hospital, they determined that my heart was alright, and we drove to the Four Corners area, where Arizona, New Mexico, Colorado, and Utah come together. It's quite an experience to be standing, high in the mountains, and seeing four states from one spot.

From there we went to Colorado Springs to visit my sister, Virginia, and her family, and to visit the Air Force Academy. After Colorado Springs, we headed home, driving across Kansas, Missouri, Illinois, and Tennessee before arriving back home in North Carolina.

Then we got settled in, as an old retired, married couple, and we did what everyone else did; we loafed. We got active in our church, joined some fellowship groups, ate a lot of food, and just plain acted like we were retired.

The next two chapters of the book are about what Mary and I have been doing in the past 21 years.

Chapter 18

TRAVELING – 1994------

To Europe

In 1997, Wolfgang Maus, Ursula's nephew, came from Germany to visit us. He and his wife and two children had been in Florida for a few weeks, and they stopped to visit us on their way home. We had a nice visit, and while they were here they invited us to come to Germany and visit them. I told them that we would like to come, but we didn't have the money to make such a long trip. Wolfgang walked over to Mary, stood in front of her, and said, "Mary, you don't pay any attention to Uncle Carl. I will pay for everything. You come and visit us."

So the next summer we flew to Germany and spent two weeks visiting with them, and doing some sightseeing. Mary had never been to Europe, so it was all new to her. In addition to spending time in Wiesbaden with them and looking over the countryside, we did such things as a cruise on the Rhine River, took a trip to their condo in the Black Forest, and visiting the Neuschwanstein Castle, southwest of Munich. That castle has been listed as one of the 20 most beautiful castles in the world. We also visited the ancient city of Heidelberg, and toured the Castle of Heidelberg. All in all, it was a wonderful trip, and we will always be grateful to Wolfgang for making that wonderful adventure possible.

Over the years, we have made two other trips to Europe, each time stopping in Germany on our way to and from Sweden. To find out why we went to Sweden, go to Chapter 19 and read about my genealogy studies of our families. Some of the most interesting things about going to Sweden were the stops along the way. Each time we flew from Greensboro to Atlanta, then from Atlanta to Frankfurt, Germany, and returned over the same route.

The first time over there we traveled by train from Frankfurt to Amsterdam, Holland, and had a very nice, seven-day bus trip through Holland, Belgium and Luxembourg. Then we flew from Amsterdam to Molmo, Sweden, rented a car, and drove to Ronneby, on the very southern tip of Sweden. That's where my father was born and where many members of his family still live. After a week and a half visiting with the family, in the Ronneby area, we drove to Copenhagen, Denmark, and then flew home to Greensboro, with transfers in Frankfurt and Atlanta.

One of the great experiences of our trips to Sweden was the drive over/thru the Oresund bridge/tunnel that connects Denmark and Sweden. It is 16 kilometers long and is about a 15 minute drive. The tunnel is for both road and rail travel. I suggest that you look it up on the internet.

The second time, we went from Greensboro to Copenhagen, via Atlanta and Frankfurt. In Copenhagen we rented a car, and drove to Malmo, where we began our visiting with Mary's family. This trip took us to several towns in south-central Sweden, and as far Northeast as Stockholm. It was a grand trip, and we met some very wonderful people. An interesting thing about Scandinavia; in the summertime, the sun sets about 11 o'clock at night, and comes up again about 2 o'clock in the morning. The day we left Stockholm we got up about 3 AM and left Stockholm in broad daylight, arriving in Copenhagen before dark.

On the way back we stopped to see Wolfgang and Angelica for a few days. While we were there, Wolfgang took his son Max, and me, on a train trip to Berlin, where we toured the city for three days.

The highlight of the trip was our visit to the site of the "Berlin Wall," and seeing the Brandenburg Gate. Wow. There is so much history at that place. We spent several hours in a museum, looking at the pictures and artifacts that demonstrated the suffering that took place during the Russian occupation.

We highly recommend Europe as a place to visit. Wherever we went, the people were nice to us, and most of them speak English. English is rapidly becoming the world language, and most of the people in Europe, who are under 50 years of age, are fluent in the language.

To Florida

In January 1995, we took the trailer and spent about a month wandering around Florida. We went down the East Coast, all the way to Key West, and came back as far as Englewood, on the West Coast. Mary had some old friends from Illinois living in Englewood, and we stopped to visit them for a couple days. They were very happy there, in their beautiful home in the nice warm weather of Central Florida. While we were there we decided to take a look around to see if we could find a place to rent for the next winter. They took us out to Englewood Beach on Manesota Key, to show us where they had vacationed in their early days in Florida. While we were there we looked at some condos on the beach, and rented a one-bedroom efficiency condo, about 20 feet from high tide, for the month of January 1996. We have been going to that condo complex every year since then, and after a few years we expanded our stay to include February. We plan to go back again next year.

To the Northeast

We have made several trips to New England over the years, usually driving as far as Maine and one time we went to Brunswick, Canada. We love the New England area and the people there and we always enjoy going back.

To the Midwest

We have been to several high school reunions at University High School in Champaign, Illinois. Mary spent four great years at Uni Hi before she went across town to the University of Illinois. We also attended my 50th class reunion in 1996 in East Chain, Minnesota and have made several other visits to East Chain..

To California

Every year we fly to San Diego, California and spend two weeks visiting with Mary's daughter Kathy Crouse, and her family.

To Minnesota and Beyond

One summer, we went to visit my relatives in southern Minnesota, then drove north, past Lake Superior, through the iron mining country of northern Minnesota and then crossed over into Canada. Once into Canada, we headed west for a while, then turned south, crossed the border into North Dakota, and drove on to Devils Lake. From Devils Lake we went south to Sheyenne, and drove down the same street where I had been in 1948. (See Chapter 8) That street had seven saloons on it, and I found the one that I had hung out in. As it happened, it was a Sunday morning, and the doors to the saloon were open and a young woman was cleaning up the place. I jumped out of the car, trotted across the street, and into the saloon. I just stood there in the middle of the room, looking around, and remembering the days of the past. That saloon looked exactly like it did in 1948. I talked to the cleaning lady and when I told her my story, she looked at me and just shook her head.

Chapter 19

HOBBIES & COMMUNITY SERVICES

MARY

Music

Mary has a beautiful soprano voice, and has been singing in church choirs since she was 8 years old. The Choir at Clemmons United Methodist Church is still a big part of Mary's life. She has sung at weddings and funerals countless numbers of times over the years, and does a great job on "God Bless America" on patriotic occasions. She can still rattle the windows on the high notes, even at age 85.

She sang with the Sweet Adelines, both chorus and quartets, until she retired from that a few years ago, not because her voice failed, but because she was too busy doing other things.

Volunteering

She has volunteered at Baptist Hospital in Winston-Salem for nearly 20 years, mostly caring for babies in the Brenner Children's Hospital. She recently received an award for 2000 hours of volunteer service.

She has been active in the United Methodist Women in our church since we joined in 1994. She has been President of that organization for most of the years that we have been members there.

Since 2009 she has been an active member of the Women's Auxiliary of the Veterans of Foreign Wars, Post 9010, in Clemmons. The Auxiliary is an official VFW organization, made up of wives, widows, and descendants of VFW members. They perform many duties alongside of the VFW members, plus many charitable activities that they do on their own. Several of the members also work at the BINGO games described below.

CARL

Veterans of Foreign Wars (VFW)

In 2001, I joined VFW Post 9010 in Clemmons, North Carolina. Following are some of the things that I have done at the VFW.

Post 9010 is the home of the VFW Memorial Honor Guard, a unit that presents military honors at veteran's funerals in a four-county area. At one point, that Honor Guard participated in over 150 funerals in a year.

Also, the Color Guard, made up of men from within the Honor Guard, performs at many ceremonies, such as presentations of the colors, marching in parades and sporting events, and honoring veterans at various locations such as schools and civic organizations.

From 2001 to 2012 I performed with both units at most of their ceremonies. I was the Commander for one year, and the Coordinator for ten years.

In 2013 I retired from the Honor Guard, primarily because I could no longer handle the cold and the heat extremes under which we performed.

Working with this honor guard is the most rewarding thing that I have ever done.

Another activity that I have been involved in since I joined the VFW is a BINGO game, every Thursday night. These BINGO games, which are open to the public, attract between 100 and 150 players each week. Proceeds from the games help support veterans causes in our community. This is a nonprofit organization and all of the workers, both VFW members and VFW Ladies Auxiliary members work, without pay, for about five hours each Thursday night.

Genealogy

During the past 20 years, I've become very interested in genealogy. I've written many books, on the subject, none of which have been published. I've found that, unless you are famous, there is no interest in genealogy within the publishing business, so I have printed copies, using my computer and printer, and distributed them as I wished. I've conducted genealogical studies on over twenty families, even that of Mark Twain. Twain's real name was Samuel Clemments, and one of the Clemmons clan tried to convince me that he was an ancestor of the founder of the town of Clemmons, NC. I couldn't make the connection.

Following are summaries of some of my genealogy studies.

On our first trip to Minnesota, in 1994, I visited with one of my cousins, Danny Whitman, and he told me about the research that he was doing on the genealogy of the Whitman family, my mother's ancestors. He told me that he had traced the genealogy of his grandfather, all the way back to 1614. That really got me interested in genealogy. I obtained a copy of the genealogy program called, "Family Tree Maker," made up a file on the Whitman family and entered information that Danny had given me.

That got me started on something that has kept me busy and happy ever since. I've traced the ancestry of Dell Whitman, my great-grandfather, through Bigod Eggleston, who had emigrated from England to America in 1614. Then I went beyond 1614, all the way to Emperor Charlemagne, who lived in 750 AD, in what is now Germany. That computer file contains over 20,000 names, and, when printed, occupies nearly a shelf in my bookcase.

The next genealogy project was that of tracing my father's family in Sweden. Dad had told me a little about his family, but not much. He came to the United States in 1911, at the age of 16, and never went back. By searching on the Internet, I discovered an organization in southern Sweden that was working on a project to transfer local church historical records to a national archive. I sent them an email and within 24 hours, I had received a reply from them, telling me that they knew who my ancestors were. In less than a week, they had contacted a first cousin of mine, (the only one that was still living) and told him what I was trying to do. I wrote letters, send emails, and made phone calls, and in about a year, Mary and I were on an airplane, headed for Sweden. We stayed in Sweden for about two weeks, visiting many of my relatives. What a wonderful treat it was to meet those people, who hadn't even known that I existed. When we got back, I put together a book entitled, "The Family of Carl Johan Mansson," and gave a copy to each of my children.

Having had success with the tracing of my family, we decided to tackle Mary's father's family, who had also come from Sweden. During the tracing of my family, I had been in touch with a retired man, in Sweden, who was helping Americans find their families, and I sent him an email telling him about Mary's family. It didn't take him very long to pick up some information on the family, and after working with him and some other people for a couple of years we went to Sweden again, to visit her family. The outcome of this project was a book entitled, "A Study of the Lewis Jackson Family of DeKalb, Illinois, (1802-2009)"

Church Work

From 2000 to 2013, I was the Church Historian. In that capacity I gathered historical information and built a significant file of documents concerning the life of Clemmons United Methodist Church, a congregation that was first organized in the late 1700s. In 2005, I wrote and printed a 60 page book entitled, "History of Clemmons United Methodist (1780–2005)." Copies of this history are now located in the History Room files, as well as in the homes of many of our church families. A copy was also donated to the Clemmons Historical Society.

In 2001, I was appointed to be the Chairman of the newly formed Church Columbarium Committee and I did most of the work involved in raising the money and of designing and building a columbarium, a building in which to inter the cremated remains of church members and their families. (A columbarium is an above-ground structure that serves the same purpose as a cemetery.) The plans call for two circular buildings, with burial niches for 768 persons. In comparison to traditional cemeteries, this columbarium will be a very large burial ground. The first section, containing 96 niches (two urns per niche) was completed and dedicated in 2002.

As each section is built, it is being surrounded by many trees and shrubs, to form a beautiful Garden of Memory

****

Cemetery Restoration

Beginning in 1995, Mary and I took on the task of restoring a Civil War Era cemetery that was located on the church grounds. There are a lot of legends surrounding this cemetery, but it is generally believed to be the family cemetery of Peter Clemmons, the man for whom the town was named.

During the restoration I compiled a book titled, "The People of the Eccles Family Cemetery." (The name, "Eccles Family Cemetery" was assigned by a group of searchers, a few years ago, who were attempting to locate all of the unnamed graveyards in the county.) Copies of the book were made available to the people of the church, and a copy was placed in the Clemmons branch of the Forsyth County library. I later wrote a book entitled, "In Search of a Family, A History and Genealogy of the Eccles Family Cemetery." The only copy of that book is located in the Church History Files.

As it turned out, the Eccles family was descended from some of the early pioneers of this area of North Carolina, so I started researching them. The most prominent family in the group was that of Peter Clemmons, who came to Clemmons in 1805, and for whom the village was named. I researched many other families in the area, and then selected nine families that were tied together by marriage, and printed a book entitled, "Nine Pioneer Families of the Yadkin Valley." The book has 311 pages of genealogy that covers many of the people who lived in this area from 1757 to 1900. The reason I stopped at 1900 was that the book began to get too large and also, records became less reliable. I gave a copy of that book to the Carolina Room of the Forsyth County Library. They had it hardbound, and it is now on a shelf in the library.

Civic Organizations

Over the years I've been a member of Toastmasters International and of the Mensa Society:

Toastmasters offered me a great proving ground for my public speaking abilities that were useful in both my work and my hobbies. I still speak at veteran's activities, civic organizations and in churches.

The Mensa society (the high IQ society) was mostly a social society, made up of very interesting people with very inquisitive minds.

Both of these organizations gave me a great deal of pleasure and exposure within the community.

Chapter 20

AFTERTHOUGHTS

It's been a great life. I haven't reached all of my goals yet, but I probably went farther than most people thought that I would.

You may have noticed that I didn't mention very many of my mistakes. Well, I didn't want the book to get too long, so I left out the really stupid stuff.

I hope that you never talk to anyone who really knew me, because they could really liven up the story, causing the book to be rated X, and you couldn't show it to your kids. After all, I wrote it as a motivational piece, hoping that the younger folks might benefit from it.

Well, so long for now. If we meet somewhere down the road, just smile and introduce yourself. I'll buy you a cup of coffee and we'll get acquainted

Some final thoughts:

"You can't teach old dogs new tricks," so act younger and fool everybody.

"If at first you don't succeed," try planning.

"The grass is always greener on the other side of the fence," so jump over the fence.

"Beggars can't be choosers," so quit begging and work around the problem.

"You can't take it with you," so give it to somebody who needs it.

Printed in the United States
By Bookmasters